GOD
Never Panics

GOD
Never Panics

~

He is
the
Anchor
of
Your
Soul

~

BY NATE CARTER

Treasure House

An Imprint of
Destiny Image® Publishers, Inc.
P.O. Box 310
Shippensburg, PA 17257-0310

"For where your treasure is, there will your heart be also."
Matthew 6:21

ISBN 0-7684-2959-5

For Worldwide Distribution
Printed in the U.S.A.

This book and all other Destiny Image, Revival Press, MercyPlace, Fresh Bread, Destiny Image Fiction, and Treasure House books are available at Christian bookstores and distributors worldwide.

1 2 3 4 5 6 7 8 9 / 10 09 08 07 06 05 04

For a U.S. bookstore nearest you, call
1-800-722-6774.

For more information on foreign distributors, call
717-532-3040.

Or reach us on the Internet:
www.destinyimage.com

Dedication

This book is dedicated to my loving family: Pam, my wife of over 15 years, and my three children, Nathan, Alecia, and Jonathan. They are such an incredible inspiration and gift from God.

I would also like to dedicate this book to my parents: Brad and Dee Carter. Their reflection of Christ has helped to shape my life and to show me that there is always hope.

Endorsements

"Hope eternal springs off the pages of Nate Carter's *God Never Panics.* From Nate's gentle spirit flows a stream of faith that will encourage down-and-outers, up-and-comers, and those just trying to survive in a world filled with challenges and naysayers."

Rev. Rob Hoskins, *Executive Director*
Book of Hope International

"There are times in life when hope can seem lost or, at the very least, unreachable. There are issues and events in life that can banish hope. Sometimes we question whether or not there is any hope at all. In his book, *God Never Panics,* Nate Carter shows us that in spite of life's trials and tribulations, there is reason for hope. This inspirational book offers an uplifting message and provides practical advice to bring one back to a place of assurance and hope in God and His purposes."

Mark D. Boykin, *Senior Pastor*
First Assembly of God, Boca Raton, Florida

"You are going to enjoy *God Never Panics* by Nate Carter. You will gain many insights on how to face tough times with a fresh perspective. Nate has weathered the firestorms of life with a thankful heart and has come through them as refined gold."

Jeff Swaim,
Convoy of Hope - WorldHope Project Director

Contents

Foreword

The man sat in my study just this afternoon, a blanched, pasty look on his countenance. He cried, "All is done! I have no hope! God doesn't care any longer."

This poor fellow had concluded, based on his limited spiritual eyesight, that God had just toppled off His eternal throne. I opened the Word and began to show him God's promises in every circumstance. The Holy Spirit illuminated the scriptures to his heart and he began to brighten with hope and promise. It seemed to dawn on him that no matter what, God never panics!

Say, that would make a grand title for a book! Ah, but that's what you hold in your hand at this very moment.

My friend of many years, Nate Carter, has been used of the Holy Spirit to write a marvelous book of hope for you. For a long time, it was my delight to work alongside Nate on the international radio broadcast "Revivaltime," which was aired weekly in 80 nations. I know Nate's life and character as well as his love for God. He is uniquely qualified to write this uplifting book.

Hebrews 11:6 teaches us that without faith it is impossible to please God. But "faith cometh by hearing, and hearing by the word of God" (Rom. 10:17 KJV). Nate Carter's message will make it easier for you to believe that the Lord is able to deliver you in any circumstance.

Years ago, a faithful pastor told me, "Dan, always give God the luxury of time." And he added, "You can lengthen the time God deals with you but you can never shorten it." This book will help you take advantage of divine promises and to believe them—even when it seems foolish to do so.

No, God never panics. And He just never fails!

Dan Betzer
Senior Pastor: First Assembly of God,
Ft. Myers, Florida
Executive Presbyter: General Council of the
Assemblies of God

Preface

It was a choking, garbled, sputtering effort, but my six-year-old baby brother finally got out the word, "Heeeelp!" Every clawing motion he made caused him to sink deeper beneath the ice and water. It seemed as if our favorite swimming hole had opened its jagged mouth wide to swallow him whole.

Only moments before, three of us had made it across the ice with no apparent problem or sense of danger. But when Tom, resembling a tightly bundled Eskimo, attempted to cross the ice, it was as if Old Man Winter pulled a lever opening a trap door. It was the "splash heard 'round the world."

While Tom was flailing about in the ice, my brother Mark quickly grabbed a long tree branch and extended it toward Tom. It was just long enough. Three of us huddled on one end, while Tom gripped the branch at the other end. We counted to three and heaved. As we pulled, Tom began to break a path through the ice like a North Atlantic ice-cutter. He neared shore and we grabbed his belt and fished him from the icy waters.

As we headed home, Tom wouldn't say a word. His teeth chattered. His body shivered. He resembled the Tin Man in the *Wizard of Oz* as he walked. But he wouldn't speak. He only wanted to get home.

It's not hard to see why. Freezing temperatures, wet clothes, and stinging hands and toes would rob anyone of joy.

Can you relate to my brother Tom? I think most of us can. One minute you are pleasantly enjoying familiar surroundings with a sense of adventure, then… The pink slip comes. The doctor calls. The policeman knocks on your door. The check bounces. The divorce papers are served.

Splash! The trap door of life opens and you fall into a cauldron of despair. The icy waters of doubt and fear drench you. The stinging images of regret haunt you. Hope eludes you. Your once pleasant stroll through life has suddenly caved in and you are left feeling hopeless.

Ever felt the chill of hopelessness? If so, then I'm glad you picked up this book. I wrote it with you in mind. In the midst of the troubles and trials of life, you will find hope. Like a candle shining in the darkest night, hope shines to you. God is your hope. He reaches out to lift you up when your world crashes in. In the upcoming pages of this book, I'd like to share with you—hope.

First, we will examine principles of overcoming discouragement and despair. Second, we will observe how men and women of the Bible overcame unprecedented obstacles. Third, we will uncover a treasure of encouragement found within God's sacred pages. And finally, we will discover that God has a plan and miracle for you.

At times, hope can seem elusive. If you are going through a problem or a struggle, then you know what I mean. If you're not in one today, you know as well as I—your next step might lead you to one.

My hope is that this book will leave you encouraged and uplifted. My prayer is that some word, story, verse, or thought will promote faith and provide hope for the challenges you face. God hasn't forgotten you. There is hope! God will come through! He is bigger than your problem and circumstances. Though *you* may panic…God never panics!

CHAPTER I

High Anxiety

Have you ever experienced the feeling of absolute despair where you felt trapped with "no hope at all"? At times hope can seem as elusive as a butterfly fluttering just beyond our grasp. And yet, hope is what keeps all of us hanging on, sometimes only by a thread, as we seek to make it through life's toughest challenges.

A writer named Ben Patterson tells the story of an S-4 submarine that was rammed by a merchant ship just off the coast of Massachusetts. It quickly sank into the cold dark waters of the Atlantic Ocean, trapping the entire crew. Every effort to rescue the crew failed. During one of their attempts, a deep-sea diver, struggling to free the crew, heard a faint tapping coming from the hull of the sunken sub. As he pressed himself against the side of the vessel, he recognized the tapping as Morse code. Mentally deciphering the message being tapped from within, he realized these words in the decoded message: "Is…there…any…hope?"

You may find yourself asking the same question. Is there any hope? Even while reading this book, you may be struggling to make sense of unforeseen circumstances, draining issues, and troublesome situations. The arena of life often brings discouragement, fatigue, and stress. And yet, in spite of what appears as insurmountable odds, we can climb the highest mountain, cross the largest ocean, or descend to the lowest depth if we have hope.

The power of hope will allow you to see a sapphire-blue sky in the midst of a storm. Hope can capture the fiery colors of a sunrise in the darkest of nights. Hope is as the light at the end of a dark and narrow tunnel. It is the bugle sounding, calling for reinforcements. Hope is like reaching out to lay hold of a rawhide rope as it lifts you to safety. Hope sees the invisible, feels the intangible, and achieves the impossible.

Although hope is the wind that propels us forward, it does not keep us from feeling the pressure and strain of life. Anxiety's assault can rob us of joy and leave us emotionally bankrupt.

LIFE IS STRESSFUL

If you live long enough, chances are you are going to face some storms. No one can live a life free of pain, trouble, and difficulty. We often struggle with internal emotions created by anxiety, stress, burnout, and tension. Problems and conflict are products of living in this world. Unfortunately, they cannot be avoided. In fact, the Bible says, "Many are the afflictions of the righteous, but the Lord delivers him out of them all" (Ps. 34:19 NKJV). Often we focus on "many are the afflictions" and fail to see "the Lord delivers." The pressures of life are inescapable, but the Lord delivers.

Robert Strand, in one of his recent books, shares a story that illustrates the pressure we often feel:

> It seems that three very timid women from Nashville ventured to New York City for a vacation in spite of the risk of muggings they so greatly feared. Sure enough, into their hotel elevator a rather large black man entered and when the doors closed, he commanded, "Sit down!"
>
> These three ladies immediately squatted on the floor, but nothing else happened until the elevator stopped at the lobby and the man got out. I'd venture to say that these three ladies felt some pressure!
>
> That night a dozen red roses awaited them in their room. A card explained, "Please accept these flowers and my apology. You must not have seen my dog when I told it to 'sit.' I was embarrassed and did not know what to do, so I just got off. I'm sorry." The card was signed "Reggie

Jackson." (For the non-baseball fan, Jackson formerly played outfield for the New York Yankees.)[1]

As that anecdote illustrates, we are constantly confronted with the pressures of life—which are sometimes made worse by our own fearful imaginations.

I grew up in Mississippi where life seemed simple and, I am sure, moved at a much slower pace than much of the United States. The pressure cooker society of the world outside my area seemed very distant. In those days the people I knew didn't take medication, or other alternatives, to relieve the stress from their daily routine.

Stress is certainly a disease of our modern times. Our convenience stores and pharmacies are filled with antacids and pain relievers to help us cope, and the revenue generated from these pharmaceuticals is astounding. Many of us have adapted and are accustomed to the pressure and stress in the metropolitan jungle.

Dr. Tom Holmes and Dr. Richard Rahe, of the University of Washington Medical School, have developed a scale for measuring the stress value of life-changing events—moving, divorce, death, having children, etc.—assigning corresponding point values to each event. Holmes and Rahe then followed their subjects' progress for two years and found that anyone undergoing significant life change became prone to illness. Patients were at greater risk for illness if their life-change score was higher than average. It didn't matter if the change was good or bad; the change itself brought stress.

In 1997, the American Heart Association's journal, *Arteriosclerosis, Thrombosis, and Vascular Biology,* reported that stress has a direct correlation with a person's health. Specifically, men who expressed high levels of despair showed a 20 percent greater increase in atherosclerosis (the narrowing of the arteries, which leads to strokes and heart attacks) than the men in the study who were optimistic. Regarding those findings, Susan Everson, a research scientist at the Human Population Laboratory of the Public Health Institute in Berkeley, California, says, "This is the same magnitude of increased risk that one sees in comparing a pack-a-day smoker to a nonsmoker."[2] In other words, stress and despair can be as bad for you as smoking a pack a day!

Stress, anxiety, worry, tension, pressure, and even changes in life's routine can contribute to the deterioration of your health and at the same time cultivate the feeling of hopelessness. It's important to take the right kind of steps in order to relieve the pressure and stress before it builds up to dangerous levels in your life.

ENCOURAGING YOURSELF IN GOD

David knew pressure. In the Book of First Samuel we read an account where David and his men returned to their camp in Ziklag to find it burned to the ground. All of their women and children, both young and old, were taken captive. Their wives, their sons, their daughters, and everything they held dear was taken. The Bible records this: "David and his men wept aloud until they had no strength left to weep" (1 Sam. 30:4).

Have you ever been there? Can you relate? Has your world ever come crashing in? Have you ever heard the doctor say "cancer"? Have you ever watched the casket of a loved one lowered into a grave? Have you ever watched your business collapse? Have you ever felt the pain of a spouse's departure? Have you ever found yourself weeping until you had no more strength left to weep?

To make matters worse, David's men were thinking of killing him. They wanted to stone him for their deep loss. In fact, the Bible records that David's men were extremely bitter. The blame landed upon David's shoulders.

Now that is pressure! What would you do? How would you respond? Notice how David faced this challenge: "David encouraged himself in the Lord his God" (1 Sam. 30:6c KJV).

Bob Benson, struggling with cancer, said, "When life caves in, you do not need reasons—you need comfort. You do not need some answers—you need someone. And Jesus does not come to us with an explanation—He comes to us with His presence."[3]

David's hope was in God. He found strength and sustenance in the sovereign Lord. He knew the only way to cope with the pain and continuing crisis was to turn to God. He bathed himself in the pool of His presence. He lived his life in the shadow of the Almighty. David found solace underneath his Father's sheltering wing.

Waiting upon God and living in His presence—these are the spiritual actions that will resurrect hope within you as it also increases your faith. The Bible says, "Those who hope in the Lord will renew their strength. They will soar on wings like eagles; they will run and not grow weary, they will walk and not be faint" (Isa. 40:31). It's in our moments of crisis that we feel God's arms surround us. When our world crumbles, we learn that He alone holds us. In moments of despair, He embraces us. In moments of hopelessness, He never lets go of us.

Some years ago on a hot summer day in southern Florida, a little boy decided to go for a swim in the old swimming hole behind his house. In a hurry to dive into the cool water, he ran out the back door, leaving behind shoes, socks, and shirt as he went. He dove into the water, not realizing that as he swam toward the middle of the lake, an alligator was swimming toward him.

His mother, in the house looking out the window, saw the tragedy that was about to occur. In utter fear, she ran toward the water, yelling to her son as loudly as she could. Upon hearing her voice, the little boy became alarmed and made a U-turn to swim to his mother. It was too late. Just as he reached her, the alligator reached him. From the dock, the mother grabbed her little boy by the arms just as the alligator snatched his legs. That began an incredible tug-of-war between the two. The alligator was much stronger than the mother, but the mother was much too passionate to let go.

A farmer happened to drive by and heard her screams. Pulling a rifle from his truck, he took aim and shot the alligator. Remarkably, after several weeks in the hospital, the little boy recovered, although his legs were extremely scarred by the vicious attack of the alligator.

A newspaper reporter who interviewed the boy after the trauma asked if he would show him his scars. The boy lifted his pant legs. And then, with obvious pride, he said to the reporter, "But look at my arms!" On his arms were deep scratches where his mother's fingernails dug into his flesh in her effort to hang on to the son she loved. The little boy added, "I have great scars on my arms because my mom wouldn't let go!"

The hands that carved out the ocean and measured the sky are the same hands that will hold you today. The hands that laid the foundation of the earth and constructed the mountains defend you today. The hands that placed the planets into orbit and leveled the plains protect you today. The hands that were nailed to a cross are the same hands that will comfort you and wipe away your tears. The hands that hold everything together are the hands that will never let you go.

David's turning point in his crisis was "encouraging himself in the Lord."

PRINCIPLES THAT WILL LEAD YOU TO THE DOOR OF HOPE

Principle #1—Don't trust in yourself; trust in God. When faced with an earth-shattering crisis, many of us panic. It is a very natural reaction. We sense our inability and lack of resources to overcome the problem. Seeking to find a solution for the impossible we quickly discover that our efforts are in vain. At some point we must recognize that God alone is sufficient to meet our needs.

Has it ever crossed your mind that God never panics? Have you ever considered that He is not sweating the circumstances? I learned as a child, in Sunday school, a little song that simply says, "God will make a way for me." I've found the message of that song to be an undeniable truth throughout my life. God will make a way in your life if you will trust Him. The Bible is clear, "Trust in the Lord with all your heart, and lean not on your own understanding; in all your ways acknowledge Him, and He shall direct your paths" (Prov. 3:5-6 NKJV).

In the book entitled *E.M. Bounds on Prayer,* E.M. Bounds writes:

> Trust sees God doing things here and now....It rises to a high place and looks into the invisible and the eternal. It realizes that God has done things and regards them as being already done. Trust brings eternity into the history and happenings of time. It transforms hope into the reality of fulfillment and changes promise into present possession.[4]

David trusted God! He made God a part of the equation. The Bible says more than once that "David inquired of the Lord." We find this pattern throughout David's life. In First Samuel 30:8 and in Second Samuel 2:1; 5:19; and 21:1 we read that "David inquired of the Lord." In First Chronicles 14:10 we find the phrase, "David inquired of God." David understood the value of seeking God and asking of Him something great.

In *There's Hope for the Future,* Richard Lee tells a true story of an incident in the life of Napoleon that illustrates the value of asking for something great.

Napoleon and his soldiers overcame an island in the Mediterranean Sea. They had fought for many days to take the island and finally succeeded. After the capture of the island at the price of many lives, Napoleon and his generals gathered for a celebration. As they were sitting around a great table, talking about the victory, they were interrupted by a young officer.

"Let me see Napoleon," he insisted to the guards. But the guards would not let him through. Finally Napoleon himself was so disturbed by the interruption that he told the guards to allow the young man to enter the tent where he was seated, and that he would speak to him personally. The young officer walked into the tent and stood at the end of the table. Looking down the table toward Napoleon, he stood in silence.

Napoleon looked at him and said, "What do you want?"

The young man looked at Napoleon and said, "Give me this island!"

The generals began to laugh. They could not believe he was forward enough to ask Napoleon for the island that they had fought so hard to win. They thought to themselves, *Who does he think he is?* Anyone with the audacity to make such a request of Napoleon was certainly putting his own life at risk.

But then Napoleon turned to one of his aides and asked for a pen and paper. He wrote out a deed to the island, signed it, and gave it to the young man, leaving his generals stunned and amazed.

"How could you do it?" one of the generals asked Napoleon. "What made him worthy to receive this great island?"

"I gave him this island," Napoleon replied, "because he honored me by the magnitude of his request."[5]

The reason David saw a great miracle was that he asked of God something great. Unfortunately, too many times, we allow our lives to drift upon the sea of life failing to unfurl the sail or set the rudder. We submit to the concept of "What will be, will be." We surrender to the "whim of fate." David, however, opened his sails and set his rudder in preparation for a miracle. David knew that God was the force that would guide his ship to victory. And so, David sought and asked of the Lord something great.

Principle #2—Don't look at circumstances; look to His Word. It is easy for us to become distracted by overwhelming circumstances. If we are not careful, our *impression* of a crisis can become bigger than the crisis itself really is and then obscure the presence of God in our lives. It is important to keep in focus that God is greater than our circumstances. God's Word renews our perspective and gives us needed insight to help us through the crisis.

After he "inquired of the Lord," David received instruction from the Lord: "Pursue them!" In addition, God revealed His plan for the outcome, "You will certainly overtake them and succeed in the rescue" (1 Sam. 30:8). Hearing God's Word brought confidence to David and energized the weary leader. The closer David grew to God, the bigger God became. The more he waited on the Lord, the more he understood the weight of God's power.

> *"No weapon forged against you will prevail, and you will refute every tongue that accuses you. This is the heritage of the servants of the Lord, and this is their vindication from Me," declares the Lord* (Isaiah 54:17).

Every giant is dwarfed and every roar is silenced in the presence of God. Who can measure the strength and power of the Almighty? Who can match His greatness? If God be for you, then who can be against you? Be encouraged that the Lord is on your side. This is the heritage of the child of God.

Principle #3—Don't run...respond. For many of us, our initial response to conflict is to withdraw. In fact, Gary Smalley says that we withdraw 85 percent of the time.[6] Unfortunately, some have the underlying impression that the problem will simply disappear. Others view their conflict as a hopeless inevitability.

Though David was at wits' end, his hope and faith in God had not diminished. Notice David's action steps. First we see David putting Principle #1 into action by seeking and trusting in God: "And David inquired of the Lord" (1 Sam. 30:8). Then we see David putting Principle #2 into action by looking to the word of the Lord. The Lord told David to "Pursue them…you will certainly overtake them and succeed in the rescue" (1 Sam. 30:8). Now David is about to put Principle #3 into action …responding to the word of the Lord. The Bible records that "David pursued" (1 Sam. 30:10 NKJV).

Hope is the soil in which the seed of faith germinates. It's the foundation upon which faith is built. As a result of his hope in God, David's faith has taken root. He puts faith into action and pursues the enemy. James says, "Faith by itself, if it is not accompanied by action, is dead" (James 2:17). It is important to be a doer of the word…to put faith into action.

During the Civil War, in July 1861, Jefferson Davis sent General Robert E. Lee to western Virginia for the purpose of "inspection, and consultation on the plan of campaign."[7] Lee's first priority was to stop in western Virginia at the headquarters of General William W. Loring. While there, Lee learned of Loring's proposed strategy to drive back the Union forces. A.L. Long, who was serving on Loring's staff at the time, wrote:

> It was obvious to all those about the general that the success of the proposed movement depended upon its speedy execution.…Delay would enable the Federals to seize all the important passes on the route, and fortify them so strongly that they would effectually arrest the advance of any force.[8]

The somnolent Loring was in no hurry to advance, and Lee was unable to persuade him otherwise. As a result, the best opportunity the Confederates had in western Virginia was lost.

Often victories are lost because we fail to take advantage of the opportunities that cross our path. How often we fail to recognize these pivotal moments in our lives. Even when we do recognize these opportunities, our delay in response may cause it to slip away. Colossians 4:5b instructs us to "make the most of every opportunity."

Andrew Carnegie once said, "As I grow older, I pay less attention to what men say. I just watch what they do."[9]

Theodore Roosevelt said in a speech in Chicago, "It is hard to fail, but it is worse never to have tried to succeed."[10]

Edmund Burke once said, "It is necessary only for the good man to do nothing for evil to triumph."[11]

It always touches the heart of God when someone will take a step of faith and dare to believe for the impossible. God moves into action when He sees a committed heart. In fact, the Bible says, "The eyes of the Lord run to and fro throughout the whole earth, to show Himself strong in the behalf of them whose heart is perfect toward Him" (2 Chron. 16:9 KJV).

Are you that someone who will dare to believe God? Is your heart completely His? Will you attempt the impossible for the Almighty? God is eager to do something great for those who believe. His divine guidance will help you through the most perplexing crisis. Instead of running from the problem, respond.

After pursuing and fighting the Amalekites, the Bible records that David recovered everything the Amalekites had taken. "Nothing was missing: young or old, boy or girl, plunder or anything else they had taken. David brought everything back" (1 Sam. 30:19). What a victory! I've often wondered what would have happened if David had never pursued the Amalekites. What would have happened if he had never responded to God's direction?

I can still hear my mother telling my three brothers and me, "God will restore to us the years that the cankerworm hath eaten." (See Joel 2:25 KJV.) At times this would be her motto. She understood that God would not forsake or abandon His people.

When it looks like all is lost, trust God. When it seems as if you are the only one fighting, trust God. When the circumstances appear to be overwhelming and impossible, trust God. I realize that there are times when life is harsh and hope is fleeting. But God is greater!

David encouraged himself in the Lord. Why not do the same? It's never too late to begin to do what is right. Trust God for the impossible. There is hope!

CHAPTER 2

God Doesn't Take Tylenol

If you're a sports enthusiast, then you immediately recognize the sights and sounds of baseball. The crack of a bat, the smell of hot dogs, and the slap of a ball sinking into a leather glove create wonderful images that excite our passion for the game. If you have followed baseball for any length of time, it is quite possible that the name *Yogi Berra* rings a bell.

In 1973, Yogi Berra led the New York Mets from last place to win the National League pennant. What was so amazing is that he accomplished this in the final month of the season. It was at that time when he spoke those enduring words, "It ain't over till it's over." I learned a similar saying in the world of music that echoes the same motif, "It's not over till the fat lady sings." As a youngster, I was often told, "You shouldn't count your chickens before they're hatched." These clever phrases remind us that the outcome of a situation may end up completely different than our circumstances suggest.

There are those times in life when it appears that all is lost. In other words, if we tried to anticipate the outcome from looking at the circumstances, we would conclude that all is hopeless. Thomas Paine referred to such difficulties as those "times that try men's souls." Each of us can relate to the suffocating feeling of being outnumbered or surrounded—where the odds are against us and probability is not in our favor. We've watched the flame of hope fading to a flicker because of what appears to be overwhelming circumstances.

During World War II, England was becoming desperate. Heavy bombing by the Germans brought despair and discouragement to the

English people, especially the youth. In an address to the students at Harrow School in October 1941, Winston Churchill gave the shortest, yet greatest, speech of his career. He rose from his chair and walked to the podium and said, "Never give in, never give in, never, never, never, never—in nothing, great or small, large or petty—never give in except to convictions of honor and good sense."[12] No matter how bad the circumstances may appear—never give in.

It may be that you recently lost a job that leaves your family desperate. The barrage of harassing calls from creditors is beginning to take its toll. It may be that you are facing a marriage that is falling apart. The temptation to leave haunts you day and night. You may find yourself in a crisis through no fault of your own created by circumstances beyond your control. You may find yourself in a troubling situation as a result of a poor or ill-advised choice. Whatever it may be, you see no way out. Your back is against the wall, and there appears to be no light at the end of the tunnel. Your circumstances appear hopeless. Hear these words: Never give in, never give in, never, never, never—there's hope.

Jesus says, "With men it is impossible, but not with God; for with God all things are possible" (Mark 10:27 NKJV). From our human perspective, every avenue seems to lead to a dead end. Every effort appears to end in failure. Our eyes are dim to the process God has put into motion for a miracle. It all funnels down to this one question, "Do we trust God?" It's at this critical moment when we must decide, is our problem bigger than God or is God bigger than our problem?

I've learned through the years that God chooses to take us through a process in order to accomplish a miracle. God could have kept Daniel from the lion's den, but rather He chose to keep the lions from eating Daniel in the lion's den. God could have kept the Hebrew children from the fiery furnace, but the greater miracle was keeping the fire from burning His faithful servants.

God sometimes chooses to allow us to reach a point of impossibility to reveal to us that He is the God who does the impossible. In this way, we discover the greatness of God. And even if we walk through the valley of the shadow of death, we will fear no evil; for God (who is bigger than any problem) is with us (see Ps. 23:4). It is important to keep in perspective that God is bigger than the circumstances that trouble us.

I traveled many years as director of the music group "Frontline," which sang weekly on the international radio broadcast called "Revivaltime." One particular tour took us to the edge of the Great Plains to the city of Colorado Springs. We all anticipated seeing the area's number one attraction, Pike's Peak. I can still recall seeing from a distance the silhouette of that incredible mountain. Many miles away, traveling toward the summit, I held up my hand and covered up the peak with my thumb. As we drove closer, the mountain seemed to swell to incredible proportions. When we reached the base of the mountain, we couldn't help but stand in awe at its size. It was mammoth! This majestic mountain, with its beautiful snow-capped peak, towered more than 14,000 feet into the deep blue sky.

Here's the point: Despite the fact that Pike's Peak had seemed small from a distance, it had always been huge. It had never changed. Only our perspective had changed. The closer we got to Pike's Peak, the bigger it seemed to become. The same is true with God. The closer we get to God, the bigger He becomes.

Hope's Hall of Fame

To lose hope is extremely dangerous. It will destroy a person physically, mentally, and spiritually. It has been said, "We can live 40 days without food, 8 days without water, 4 minutes without air, and only a few seconds without hope." Men and women throughout the pages of Scripture, who have faced impossible odds, testify that God and God alone was their hope and ultimate refuge. They understood that God was greater than any force or foe.

Hope Hall of Famer—Paul

Can you imagine being beaten, stoned, shipwrecked, and bitten by a deadly snake—not to mention being falsely accused and imprisoned? Paul endured great hardship for the cause of Christ and yet, he counted it all joy. In Paul's letter to the Romans, we find a beautiful description of hope.

> *We know that the whole creation has been groaning as in the pains of childbirth right up to the present time. Not only so, but we ourselves, who have the firstfruits of the Spirit, groan inwardly as we wait eagerly for our adoption as sons, the redemption of our bodies. For in this hope we were saved. But hope that is seen is no hope at all. Who*

hopes for what he already has? But if we hope for what we
do not yet have, we wait for it patiently (Romans 8:22-25).

Hope Hall of Famer—Peter

Can you picture Peter reaching for a hand as he quickly sinks beneath the waves of the Sea of Galilee? Can you feel his anger as he slices off the ear of a Roman soldier? Can you hear the rooster crowing as he denies Christ for the third time? Though Peter was blanketed with failure, he became a vital link in spreading the gospel. Peter knew the source of his hope:

> *For you know that it was not with perishable things*
> *such as silver or gold that you were redeemed from the*
> *empty way of life handed down to you from your forefa-*
> *thers, but with the precious blood of Christ, a lamb without*
> *blemish or defect. He was chosen before the creation of the*
> *world, but was revealed in these last times for your sake.*
> *Through Him you believe in God, who raised Him from the*
> *dead and glorified Him, and so your faith and hope are in*
> *God* (1 Peter 1:18-21).

Hope Hall of Famer—Job

I've always been fascinated with Job. Here is a man who lost everything except hope. He was stripped of his fortune, his health deteriorated to the point of death, and he tragically lost his family. His friends cast the judgmental shroud of blame over him for his affliction. His surviving wife demanded that he curse God and die as a result of this catastrophe. And yet, he was able to express: "Though He slay me, yet will I hope in Him; I will surely defend my ways to His face" (Job 13:15).

Though his suffering and loss seemed unbearable, Job never lost hope!

Hope Hall of Famer—David

Many of us recognize David as the giant-slayer and as the man after God's own heart. We often view David as a man of super-human qualities. However, it's important to remember that David had many adversaries, fought numerous battles, often made poor choices, and struggled with family problems that usually brought him to a point of despair. Though he faced many difficulties, there is no doubt where his hope was found:

No king is saved by the size of his army; no warrior escapes by his great strength. A horse is a vain hope for deliverance; despite all its great strength it cannot save. But the eyes of the Lord are on those who fear Him, on those whose hope is in His unfailing love, to deliver them from death and keep them alive in famine. We wait in hope for the Lord; He is our help and our shield (Psalms 33:16-20).

Hope Hall of Famer—Isaiah

Although Isaiah was a prophet, he was persecuted and rejected by his very own people. His call to repentance was largely ignored. It's through this stormy period that Isaiah pens the beautiful imagery of hope:

Do you not know? Have you not heard? The Lord is the everlasting God, the Creator of the ends of the earth. He will not grow tired or weary, and His understanding no one can fathom. He gives strength to the weary and increases the power of the weak. Even youths grow tired and weary, and young men stumble and fall; but those who hope in the Lord will renew their strength. They will soar on wings like eagles; they will run and not grow weary, they will walk and not be faint (Isaiah 40:28-31).

Hope Hall of Famer—Jeremiah

Jeremiah watched in horror at the destruction of his homeland. He watched his people, whom he loved deeply, carried off into exile as a result of ignoring his persistent warnings. Through it all, Jeremiah knew the source of his hope:

Do any of the worthless idols of the nations bring rain? Do the skies themselves send down showers? No, it is You, O Lord our God. Therefore our hope is in You, for You are the one who does all this (Jeremiah 14:22).

The Bible has many examples of men and women who dared to believe God for the impossible—who found favor in a critical hour at a crossroad in life. They viewed every obstacle as an opportunity for God to perform a miracle.

GOD NEVER PANICS

It may be that right now you find yourself at a crossroad. Your circumstances appear daunting. You've caught yourself saying, "This will never work—it's impossible!" You've done the math and the calculation yields despair.

If you were to look in a thesaurus at the word *despair,* you would find: "to lose hope, lose heart, give up on hope, abandon hope, have no hope, have a heavy heart." This description could be describing you. Your heart seems heavy. You feel as though there is a 10-pound ball of lead lodged inside your chest. God seems silent and distant. You wonder to yourself, "Does God really understand?" You are haunted by the thought that you will never be happy again.

The Bible says, "Why are you downcast, O my soul? Why so disturbed within me? Put your hope in God..." (Ps. 42:5).

Be encouraged! God never panics! There is nothing that escapes His eye. He is not sleeping! He is not too busy! You won't hear Him shouting, "Angels! Why didn't someone notify Me of this problem? How did we let it get this far out of control?" You won't catch Him taking Tylenol or Advil as a result of worry and stress concerning your crisis. He is not sweating the outcome. He is not baffled or stumped at the enormity and complexity of your problem. Why?—GOD IS GREATER! He is greater than your circumstances. He is greater than your failures. He is greater than whatever life may throw at you. He will defend the defenseless and strengthen the weak. He will move a mountain, stop the sun, and divide an ocean for those who hope in Him. He is passionate about doing the impossible, the extraordinary, the inconceivable, and the unimaginable for you.

Isaiah pens a beautiful verse, which expresses the depth of God's passion and provision for us:

> *This is what the Lord says... "Fear not, for I have redeemed you; I have summoned you by name; you are Mine. When you pass through the waters, I will be with you; and when you pass through the rivers, they will not sweep over you. When you walk through the fire, you will not be burned; the flames will not set you ablaze. For I am*

the Lord, your God, the Holy One of Israel, your Savior"
(Isaiah 43:1-3a).

GOD OF THE IMPOSSIBLE

The impossible only finds a home in our mind. As time passes, it becomes permanently attached to our thoughts, dreams, and goals. At that point, only God has the ability to remove the doubt and its horrible stain. God sometimes leads us to a place of impossibility to accomplish the impossible and cure the disease of doubt.

Moses was a man who faced the impossible on many occasions. From his birth until Israel reached the Promised Land, his life was challenged with impossibilities. When I think of Moses, I can't help but picture Charlton Heston. I've often popped popcorn, poured sodas, and snuggled on the couch to watch the timeless movie, *The Ten Commandments.* My favorite part of the movie is when Moses (played by Charlton Heston) and the nation of Israel are halted at the bank of the Red Sea while Pharaoh and the Egyptian army approaches. The suspense builds and the nail biting begins as you view Moses' dilemma. Even after Moses holds out his staff and parts the sea, I am still at the edge of my chair wondering if everyone is going to make it across in time.

As I've studied the account in Exodus, I've noticed some important facts that the movie leaves out. The Bible reveals this, "So God led the people around by the desert road toward the Red Sea" (Ex. 13:18a). What a shock! I had always pictured Moses fleeing from Pharaoh and unexpectedly happening upon the Red Sea. However, the Bible is very clear: "God led" them to the Red Sea. It wasn't an accident or blunder! It wasn't a mistake or miscalculation! It wasn't even a wrong turn. God led the people to the Red Sea. Why? Why would God lead His people to a dead end?

As we continue to read, we find that *"the Lord went ahead of them in a pillar of cloud to guide them on their way and by night in a pillar of fire to give them light, so that they could travel by day or night. Neither the pillar of cloud by day nor the pillar of fire by night left its place in front of the people"* (Ex. 13:21). God not only leads them but also gives them a clear, unmistakable physical sign to guide their steps. It would appear that God is leading His people into a deadly arena with no exits. Why?

I've found myself at the bank of a "Red Sea" many times. I've often searched for a way out only to discover there was none. I've looked for where I went wrong and where I might have missed God. And yet, God led me to this place that I might discover that He is the door to a miracle. He is the portal by which I must travel to experience the blessing that He has designed. It's important to realize that God doesn't play dice with our lives or leave the outcome to chance.

If we look carefully, God was actually taking His people to a place of seeming impossibility with no way out. Sometimes the only way God can get us to a new place is to take us through a desert. It's at those moments in life that we discover how big God really is and how awesome His plans are! It's in those settings that we learn the limitless range of God's power. It's in those moments we find that God will never fail us. God wanted His people to recognize Him as the door to the possible.

THE LORD WILL FIGHT FOR YOU

I have found a verse in this passage that has given me strength in desperate times. Exodus 14:14 is like finding water in the desert. When the approach of Pharaoh and his army brought fear into the heart of God's people, Moses declared this indelible statement of faith, "The Lord will fight for you; you need only to be still" (Ex. 14:14).

Many times we don't realize who is on our side. We fail to consider the grandeur of God. The Bible says, "The heavens declare the glory of God" (Ps. 19:1). When I was in school I learned that it would only take two seconds to reach the moon if we traveled at the speed of light (186,282 miles per second). It would take eight minutes to reach the sun. In four months, at the speed of light, you would exit our solar system. Continuing at that speed, it would take five years to reach Alpha Centauri, the nearest star. It would then take 100,000 years to leave the Milky Way galaxy. If you wanted to visit the Great Nebula, the nearest galaxy, it would take you 1.5 million years if you maintained the speed of light. In fact, you could travel at that speed for 4.5 billion years and never leave the universe. Why did God create such a huge universe? He created the universe to demonstrate the breadth and magnitude of His awesome power. It certainly qualifies Him to do the impossible in our lives.

Moses is considered a man of faith because his concept of God was greater than a thousand Pharaohs and their armies. He understood the magnitude and power of the Almighty. He was able to face each day with confidence and hope because his confidence and hope was in a great God. He may not have known what tomorrow held, but he knew God held tomorrow. He recognized that the Creator of the universe held the cords of destiny in His hands.

There was a research team comprised of botanists surveying the landscape in a remote part of the Swiss Alps. They were hoping to discover new or rare flowers. As they explored the region, one of the team members spotted an isolated patch of beautiful flowers exploding with color. As they studied these rare flowers through binoculars, they determined that these were a species that had not previously been cataloged. Their excitement quickly changed to concern when they realized that being lowered into a deep ravine by a rope would be the only way to access the flowers. A Swiss lad, watching the activity, was approached by a team member and offered a large sum of money if he would allow himself to be lowered into the ravine to gather a sample of these rare flowers.

The young lad took a long look at the deep ravine and said, "Wait here, I'll be back soon," and disappeared over the mountain.

Shortly, he returned with an older stately gentleman. He approached the research team and exclaimed, "I'll be glad to go over the cliff and get the flowers if you let this man hold the rope. He's my dad!"

It makes a big difference who holds the ropes. The problems we face aren't too big; it's just that our concept of God is too small. God is the first, the last, the beginning, and the end. He always was, always is, always will be. The world can't stop Him; its armies can't defeat Him; its schools can't explain Him; its leaders can't ignore Him. Herod couldn't kill Him. The Pharisees couldn't confuse Him. Nero couldn't crush Him. Hitler couldn't silence Him. He's the power of the powerful, the Ancient of Days, the Ruler of rulers, the Leader of leaders. He is holy, mighty, and true. His ways are right, His word eternal, and His will unchanging. He is Redeemer, Savior, Lord, and King!

We may not always understand why God leads us to the "Red Seas" of life, but He is the Director and holds the script in His hands. We may not always see the purpose for the challenges we face in life, but He is in control! Remember, God doesn't take Tylenol—He doesn't have to. Don't let the seeds of doubt be sown, for God will not forsake His own. All things are possible to those who believe. Remember, "It's not over, even when the fat lady sings."

CHAPTER 3

God Doesn't Play Dice with Our Lives

How many times have you heard the phrase, "What a coincidence!" I never cease to be amazed at how a *blunder* can turn into a *blessing*. What we sometimes see as a mishap is actually a miracle. I think this story says it best:

> A shipwrecked man managed to reach an uninhabited island. There, to protect himself against the elements and to safeguard the few possessions he had salvaged, he painstakingly built a little hut from which he constantly and prayerfully scanned the horizon for the approach of a ship. Returning one evening after a search for food, he was terrified to find the hut completely enveloped in flames. Yet by divine mercy this hard affliction was changed into a mighty advantage. Early the following morning he awoke to find a ship anchored off the island. When the captain stepped ashore, he explained, "We saw your smoke signal and came." Everything the marooned man owned had to be destroyed before he could be rescued.[13]

Life is full of surprises. Sometimes these surprises bring us joy and sometimes pain. It is important to realize that with God there are no coincidences. God is not caught unaware or surprised by events that unfold in our lives. The Bible reveals that God has a divine plan for our lives: " 'For I know the plans I have for you,' declares the Lord, 'plans to prosper you and not to harm you, plans to give you hope and a future' " (Jer. 29:11).

Our perspective of God's plan for our lives can be blurred when we are faced with adversity. And yet, it's in those uncomfortable seasons of life that God is able to speak more clearly to us. C.S. Lewis writes: "God whispers to us in our pleasures, speaks in our conscience, but shouts in our pains."[14] It's through this process that God accomplishes His eternal purpose. It's through the trials and hardships of life that we are prepared for greatness. A.W. Tozer writes, "It is doubtful whether God can bless a man greatly until He has hurt him deeply."[15]

THE LORD IS WITH YOU

Joseph was a man who was hurt deeply. He was bounced around like a leaf in a windstorm. Every event that transpired in his life seemed to make no sense. It seemed to have no rhyme or reason. He was sold into slavery after his brothers became jealous of his favor with their father. He was then falsely accused and thrown into prison as a result of a failed seductive ploy by his master's wife. Later, an inmate he had helped in prison by interpreting a dream for him disregarded his request for help. During these disappointments in Joseph's life, the Bible records, *"The Lord was with him"* (Gen. 39:21a). What an encouraging phrase that should cause us to pause and take note.

The Lord was with Joseph when he felt the sting of betrayal from family. The Lord was near when the shroud of false accusations covered Joseph's life. The Lord was there when Joseph felt the claustrophobic feeling of being confined to a dungeon. The Lord was with Joseph when he felt the emptiness of being abandoned by a friend who could have aided in his release. Through each of these disappointing and discouraging events, the Lord was with Joseph.

God gives us this promise, "Never will I leave you; never will I forsake you" (Heb. 13:5b). I learned in Bible school that the Greek word translated as "never" in this verse is emphatic. It is like saying it this way, "Never, no, not ever, not by any means, in no case, not at all, not at all in any wise, nor ever will I leave you...or forsake you." No matter how difficult the problem or perplexing the circumstance, God will never abandon you.

A young mother was cleaning her home with the assistance of her seven-year-old daughter. As they were completing their tasks, the mother asked her daughter to go to the back porch and get the broom. The young girl mentioned with concern, "But Mommy, the light is not working on the back porch." The mother proceeded to explain that Jesus would be with her and not to worry. With great hesitation, the little girl went to the back porch and opened the screen door. As she peered into the darkness she thought of her mother's words that Jesus would be with her. She then spoke, "Jesus, if You are out there, would You please pass me the broom?"

There are those moments in life when we feel isolated and alone—those moments when it is difficult to see what's ahead. It is important to remind ourselves that God has not and will not abandon us. When we trust God with our lives, we must understand that He is working all things for our good and His glory. Like a candle in the dark illuminating our path, God gently guides His children. The Bible says, "In his heart a man plans his course, but the Lord determines his steps" (Prov. 16:9).

Although Joseph couldn't see it at the time, God was at work in every detail of his life. He was diligently crafting a master plan for Joseph and the nation of Israel. God, who is omniscient, saw that a catastrophic famine and drought was coming upon the earth. He needed one man who would have the power and authority to offer relief to starving nations trapped by the coming devastation. The only man with that kind of power was the Grand Vizier—the second highest executive office of ancient Egypt. The scenario was this: God needed to get Joseph, a teenager, from his father's farm in Hebron to the second most powerful position in Egypt.

Joseph must have wondered what the purpose was behind the course of events occurring in his life. After all, he had not done anything to deserve such harsh treatment from his brothers or the dark dampness of the dungeon. But he endured the experience, never compromising his faith in God. He waited with purpose—knowing God would not forsake him. As a precious treasure safely hidden, he anticipated God's hour of unveiling. Charles Swindoll writes:

> All whom God uses greatly are first hidden in the
> secret of His presence, away from the pride of man. It is

there our vision clears. It is there the silt drops from the current of our life and our faith begins to grasp His arm. Abraham waited for the birth of Isaac. Moses didn't lead the Exodus until he was eighty. Elijah waited beside the brook. Noah waited 120 years for rain. Paul was hidden away for three years in Arabia....God is working while His people are waiting, waiting, waiting. Joseph is being shaped for a significant future.[16]

I've been there! You've been there! Each of us has experienced those moments when the compass of life seems broken and we have no idea what direction to take. When the wind in the sail has stopped blowing we are left powerless. We navigate through the waters of ambiguity and uncertainty wondering if we've drifted off course. It's as if we've been put on hold. We wait, and wait, and wait. And yet, this is the passageway God has chosen to shape us for greatness. It's a part of God's design to take us to a place of grace. As a lighthouse appears to a ship in the night, so will God's blessing appear to those who wait on Him.

I've always marveled at Joseph's life. His ability to negotiate the steep slopes on the mountain of adversity has certainly been a source of inspiration. Edmund Hillary, when climbing Mount Everest, was quoted as saying, "It is not the mountain we conquer but ourselves."[17] Adversity causes us to look inward and upward. It causes us to pause and take inventory of courage. The Bible says, "It was good for me to be afflicted so that I might learn Your decrees" (Ps. 119:71). It is through these challenges and conflicts that our faith is resolved, our character is realized, and God's purpose is revealed. Thomas Paine, during the Revolutionary War, declared:

> The harder the conflict, the more glorious the triumph. What we obtain too cheap, we esteem too lightly; it is dearness only that gives everything its value....I love the man that can smile in trouble, that can gather strength from distress and grow brave by reflection. 'Tis the business of little minds to shrink; but he whose heart is firm, and whose conscience approves his conduct, will pursue his principles unto death.[18]

Joseph prevailed and endured the season of crisis. Then, suddenly, Pharaoh summoned Joseph! It had been 13 years since his brothers had sold him as a slave. It had been 13 years since he had experienced freedom, family events, a father's love, and many other memory-making opportunities. And suddenly, he is called out of his dungeon experience.

There was nothing different about the day. It was an ordinary day. It appeared to be a day much like today. He woke up and was busy about his daily tasks. He was engaged in his normal routine when, out of the blue, the guards came and announced that Pharaoh requested his presence "and they brought him hastily out of the dungeon" (Gen. 41:14a KJV). The Bible uses words like hastily, straightway, and suddenly to remind us that when God moves, He often does it quickly. That's God's way! His blessings come to us suddenly.

It may be that God's blessing comes as you open your mailbox. It may come from a phone call or via E-mail. It may come from an old friend or an estranged spouse. It may come from a family member or distant relative. It may be found in a familiar place or a strange place. It may come in the most likely or unlikely manner. On an ordinary day, suddenly, you are confronted with God's favor. Your heart of hearts tells you it's God's providence. No discouraging word or circumstance will pry this blessing from your grasp. Your miracle has just begun on a day much like today.

GOD REMEMBERS HIS OWN

In the court of Pharaoh stands a solitary figure...a mere silhouette of a man who is dwarfed in comparison to the size of an awesome global power. As he is ushered into the throne room, he is blinded by the splendor of his surroundings. Gold and pageantry announce the sophistication and advances of the Egyptian empire. Pillars of grandeur, laden with jewels, lead into a room prepared for a god. Few have ever seen the intricate beauty of the palace. Joseph's eyes dilate as he becomes accustomed to the brilliance of Pharaoh's castle. He is bathed in the aroma of incense and perfumes...a stark contrast to the rancid odor of the dungeon. Surrounding the throne are Pharaoh's advisors, officers, guards, and the familiar face of the chief cupbearer.

As Joseph's eyes pan the palace, he hears the voice of Pharaoh...

"I had a dream and no one can interpret it. But I have heard it said of you that when you hear a dream you can interpret it."

"I cannot do it," Joseph replied to Pharaoh, "but God will give Pharaoh the answer he desires."

Then Pharaoh said to Joseph, "In my dream I was standing on the bank of the Nile, when out of the river there came up seven cows, fat and sleek, and they grazed among the reeds. After them seven other cows came up—scrawny and very ugly and lean. I had never seen such ugly cows in all the land of Egypt. The lean, ugly cows ate up the seven fat cows that came up first. But even after they ate them, no one could tell that they had done so; they looked just as ugly as before, then I woke up. In my dreams I also saw seven heads of grain, full and good, growing on a single stalk. After them, seven other heads sprouted—withered and thin and scorched by the east wind. The thin heads of grain swallowed up the seven good heads. I told this to the magicians, but none could explain it to me."

Then Joseph said to Pharaoh, "The dreams of Pharaoh are one and the same. God has revealed to Pharaoh what He is about to do. The seven good cows are seven years, and the seven good heads of grain are seven years; it is one and the same dream. The seven lean, ugly cows that came up afterward are seven years, and so are the seven worthless heads of grain scorched by the east wind: They are seven years of famine.

"It is just as I said to Pharaoh: God has shown Pharaoh what He is about to do. Seven years of great abundance are coming throughout the land of Egypt, but seven years of famine will follow them. Then all the abundance in Egypt will be forgotten, and the famine will ravage the land. The abundance in the land will not be remembered, because the famine that follows it will be so severe. The reason the dream was given to Pharaoh in two forms is that the matter has been firmly decided by God, and God will do it soon.

"And now let Pharaoh look for a discerning and wise man and put him in charge of the land of Egypt. Let Pharaoh appoint commissioners over the land to take a fifth of the harvest of Egypt during the seven years of abundance. They should collect all the food of these good years that are coming and store up the grain under the authority of Pharaoh, to be kept in the cities for food. This food should be held in reserve for the country, to be used during the seven years of famine that will come upon Egypt, so that the country may not be ruined by the famine."

The plan seemed good to Pharaoh and to all his officials. So Pharaoh asked them, "Can we find anyone like this man, one in whom is the spirit of God?"

Then Pharaoh said to Joseph, "Since God has made all this known to you, there is no one so discerning and wise as you. You shall be in charge of my palace, and all my people are to submit to your orders. Only with respect to the throne will I be greater than you" (Genesis 41:15-40).

In an instant, Joseph went from the dungeon to the second most powerful person in the world. Just moments earlier, Joseph was a seemingly forgotten prisoner with no future. Now he walks the palace in royal attire. He wears a gold necklace around his neck and Pharaoh's ring upon his finger. His chariot is fashioned of the finest quality. His very word now alters the destiny of those who live throughout the nation of Egypt.

If all that had happened to me, I know what I would have been thinking: At midnight all of this will turn to pumpkins and mice. Although it seemed "too good to be true," God's blessing in Joseph's life was unmistakable! God's blessings are always grander than what we could ever imagine or think. And yet, the pit and the palace were all a part of God's unfolding plan in Joseph's life. I've heard it said, "We turn to God for help when our foundations are shaking, only to learn that it is God who is shaking them." Sometimes disappointments are God's appointments. Events and circumstances happen in our lives for a reason. It's all part of God's master plan.

A FAMILY AFFAIR

As the winds howl across barren fields, the Middle East is plunged into a season of starvation. The soil becomes parched and cracked as the sun consumes the earth. A sense of foreboding envelops the nations. Joseph was right! A plague is stretching across the landscape. Joseph's forecast of a famine has come to fruition.

Although Egypt's silos are pregnant with grain, surrounding nations are crumbling under the weight of this catastrophic famine. The people of Israel are no exception. As they struggle to survive in the burning crucible of the desert, they hear that there is plenty of food and water in Egypt. Jacob has no choice but to send his sons to Egypt to buy grain.

Joseph, as governor of Egypt, administers the selling of the grain. When his brothers approach him to buy grain, he immediately recognizes them. They, however, do not recognize him, and they bow as they request permission to purchase food. Joseph uses this as an opportunity to test his brothers. He cleverly weaves a web of suspense, intrigue, passion, and accusation into the uneventful lives of his brothers. Joseph's plan climaxes when the youngest of the brothers, Benjamin, is about to become an Egyptian slave and be separated from his brothers. Judah, makes a passionate plea to take his youngest brother's place as a slave. When Joseph hears this, he can no longer control himself and he weeps loudly. Joseph then says to his brothers:

> "*...Come close to me." When they had done so, he said, "I am your brother Joseph, the one you sold into Egypt! And now, do not be distressed and do not be angry with yourselves for selling me here, because it was to save lives that God sent me ahead of you. For two years now there has been famine in the land and for the next five years there will not be plowing and reaping. But God sent me ahead of you to preserve for you a remnant on earth and to save your lives by a great deliverance. So then, it was not you who sent me here, but God*" (Genesis 45:4-8a).

Wow! What character! What an attitude! Joseph comes to this pinnacle of his life and chooses to see God's plan instead of man's ploy. He focuses on God's investment instead of man's infractions. In essence,

Joseph is saying to his brothers, you meant it for evil, but God meant it for good.

God's point of view of our circumstances is vastly different from our point of view. Recently, I came across a story that illustrates God's point of view.

> It was my privilege a few years ago to hear Corrie ten Boom speak. She was introduced and received an ovation from the audience before she even began. She was stooped with age just a bit, dressed very humbly, in a well-worn dress. Her appearance was anything but imposing.

> She began speaking in a very soft voice rich with her Dutch accent. Corrie told of her upbringing and described her family. Then she began to tell of the war-torn years of the Second World War. It was not a pretty description. She related how her family hid and helped many Jewish people escape the persecution of the Nazi regime. It was a fascinating story. Every ear was intent so as not to miss a single detail.

> My wife and I were sitting about two-thirds of the way back in the auditorium of a couple thousand people. I had not noticed why Miss ten Boom had her head down much of the time. At first I thought she was looking very carefully at her notes. But then I paid closer attention and discovered that as she was speaking, she was working on a piece of needlepoint.

> Miss ten Boom took us on a journey to her time spent in the concentration camp. It was a sordid tale of the cruelty of human beings to other human beings. She moved on to her moment of release—her sister had died, her father had died. It was a moving moment as she began to wrap up her story.

> Corrie explained that none of us has the privilege in life to see what is really happening or why things have to happen like they do. Then she held up the needlepoint for us to see. It was about 10 by 14 inches or so, and in a frame.

She showed us the backside. It was nothing but a jumble of threads and colors with no discernible pattern. She explained that this is how we see our lives—a view from the bottom, a view that may make no sense. Then she turned her needlework over and showed us the finished side. The pattern and the colors made a beautiful scene. All the threads showed their purpose.

Corrie then concluded: "This is how God views your life and someday we will have the privilege of viewing it from His point of view."[19]

God has always been behind the scenes like a puppet-master, pulling the strings. He has always been in control. You and I are not at this point in our journey by accident. Despite the enemy's best effort to destroy, defame, diminish, and discourage, God never takes His hand off those who trust Him. He is raising you up to fulfill His purpose. Remember, "The steps of a good man are ordered by the Lord" (Ps. 37:23a KJV). No matter how bad the circumstances may seem, trust God. God always has a plan. His design is perfect. God does not play dice with our lives.

CHAPTER 4

A Whale of a Tale

It was a cool February morning in the year 1891 when a young English sailor named James Bartley set sail with the crew of the whaling ship *Star of the East,* in the waters off the Falkland Islands in the South Atlantic. This voyage would soon prove to be an "adventure in odyssey" as James prepared for a normal season at sea.

One day, about three miles offshore, quite suddenly, the whalers spotted a sperm whale that later proved to be 80 feet long and weighed some 80 tons! Two boats with crew members and harpooners—one of them was Bartley—were sent out to get the whale. As they closed in, one harpooner catapulted his eight-foot spear toward the whale. The instant it struck, the whale twisted and lashed out with its huge tail. The tail slammed into one rowboat, lifted it into the air, and capsized it. But the sailors soon subdued and killed the wounded mammal.

When the rowboat was righted, Bartley and another crewman were missing and written off as drowned. The crew pulled the carcass of the whale alongside the ship and worked until midnight removing the blubber. The next morning, using a derrick, the sailors hoisted the whale's stomach on deck.

According to M. de Parville, science editor of *The Journal des Debats,* who investigated the incident, there

45

was movement inside the whale's belly. When it was opened, Bartley was found on the inside, unconscious. He was carried on deck and bathed in sea water. He was confined to the captain's quarters for two weeks, because he was acting like a lunatic.

Within four weeks, Bartley fully recovered and related what it had been like to live in the belly of the whale. For the rest of his life, Bartley's face, neck and hands remained white, bleached by the whale's gastric juices![20]

RUNNING FROM GOD

Have you ever considered the thought of being swallowed by a whale? I don't know about you, but sliding down the digestive tract of a large marine leviathan has to rate high on the stress scale. I can't think of anything more claustrophobic and terrifying. It sounds like something from a Stephen King movie. And yet, the Bible describes such an event.

God told Jonah, "Go to the great city of Nineveh and preach against it, because its wickedness has come up before Me" (Jon. 1:2).

This was not what Jonah wanted to hear. His prejudice toward Nineveh could not be hidden. This metropolis, known for its impaling style of executions, was on Jonah's top 10 most hated places. It was a brutal and savage society made infamous by its extreme cruelty. And God told Jonah to "go...and preach against it."

> *But Jonah ran away from the Lord and headed for Tarshish. He went down to Joppa, where he found a ship bound for that port. After paying the fare, he went aboard and sailed for Tarshish to flee from the Lord* (Jonah 1: 3).

Choice, not chance, determines destiny. In other words, the choices you and I make have an impact on our future.

This is certainly the case with Jonah. His decision to disobey and run from God is premeditated and deliberate. It's this decision that will linger in his mind and taunt his soul. So, Jonah runs to a port, buys a ticket, boards a ship, and sails to Tarshish in an effort to escape God's purpose and plan.

How foolish we are to think that we can run from God. Think about it. What place would be so far away that God couldn't see us? What depth would be so deep that God couldn't reach us? What place would be so dense that God couldn't find us? What place would be so high that God couldn't touch us? But still, we play hide and seek with God. We often run from His will, His call, and His plan for our lives. It's in the process of running that we soon find ourselves entangled in the web of adversity. Billy Graham said, "It is the absence of the knowledge of God and man's refusal to obey Him that lies at the root of every problem that besets us."[21]

Could it be that you've been running from God? Could it be that the struggles you are facing are the result of a choice to flee from God? This would certainly prove to be Jonah's testimony. It was Jonah's refusal to obey God that became the foundation for trouble.

"Then the Lord sent a great wind" (Jon. 1:4a), which was so fierce that even the seasoned sailors became terrified. The crew, being superstitious, sought for an answer by casting lots. And—would you believe it?—the lot fell on Jonah. Jonah then explained to the crew that if they would throw him into the sea, the tempest would cease. So, the crew did what Jonah had requested and immediately the wind and the sea became calm.

As Jonah began to sink beneath the waves, "the Lord provided a great fish to swallow Jonah, and Jonah was inside the fish three days and three nights" (Jon. 1:17).

LIFE INSIDE A WHALE

Now, I've heard of being "in a pickle," "in a pinch," "in a jam," and "in hot water." But Jonah, the prophet of God, finds himself being "in a whale." His choices have led him to this sobering moment of peril. Although he is completely drenched, he can still feel the chilling sweat of distress. His mind is bathed in the horror of dying inside the whale. He is eating the bitter herb of hopelessness as he considers "if only." As Winston Churchill once expressed, "The terrible 'ifs' accumulate."[22] John Greenleaf Whittier writes, "For of all sad words of tongue or pen, the saddest are these: 'It might have been!' "[23]

Have you ever fallen prey to the relentless feeling of regret? Have you ever wanted to reverse a decision? Have you ever felt the continuous sting of a poor choice? Jonah did. Jonah felt the highest levels of hopelessness. And to top it off, Jonah knew that he had only himself to blame. He confessed, "I know that it is my fault" (Jon. 1:12).

It had been Jonah's desire to get as far away from God as possible. He would spare no expense and travel any distance to run and hide from God. It's a bit of poetic justice that God would put Jonah in a place that seemed beyond the boundaries of His reach. God allowed Jonah to go further than even Jonah intended. And yet, in the dark, obscure surroundings of the digestive tract in the belly of a whale, near the bottom of a murky sea, God was found. Corrie ten Boom often said, "There is no pit so deep but He is not deeper still."[24]

SALVATION COMES FROM THE LORD

"From inside the fish Jonah prayed" (Jon. 2:1a). Trouble often drives men and women to God in prayer. Jonah is no exception. He values the strength and promise that prayer offers. Even in the depths of despair, his heart seeks God. His thoughts of God release a ray of hope, which brightens his dark circumstances. He understands that prayer makes a difference.

John Bunyan once said, "You can do more than pray after you have prayed, but you cannot do more than pray until you have prayed."[25]

God's Word encourages us with these words, "This is the confidence we have in approaching God: that if we ask anything according to His will, He hears us. And if we know that He hears us—whatever we ask—we know that we have what we asked of Him" (1 John 5:14-15).

God says, "Call to Me and I will answer you and tell you great and unsearchable things you do not know" (Jer. 33:3).

And so it was from inside the fish that Jonah prayed:

> *In my distress I called to the Lord, and He answered me. From the depths of the grave I called for help, and You listened to my cry.... The engulfing waters threatened me, the deep surrounded me; seaweed was wrapped around my head. To the roots of the mountains I sank down; the earth beneath barred me in forever. But You brought my life up from the pit, O Lord my God...Those*

who cling to worthless idols forfeit the grace that could be theirs. But I, with a song of thanksgiving, will sacrifice to You. What I have vowed I will make good. Salvation comes from the Lord (Jonah 2:2, 5-6, 8-9).

Jonah reaches a turning point...a moment of truth...a realization of his need for God. He anchors on to what he knows to be true of God rather than the inconsistency of his emotions and present situation. Instead of running from God, we find Jonah running to God. Jonah not only knows the faithfulness, compassion, and mercy of God, but he understands His ways. Jonah concludes his prayer by saying, "Salvation comes from the Lord."

Salvation indeed comes from the Lord. In the midst of an alarming crisis, God is near. When we are swallowed in the depths of despair, God is a prayer away. It doesn't matter how far you've gone or how troubling your circumstances. The Bible says, "God is...an ever-present help in trouble" (Ps. 46:1). Even when we find ourselves in a quandary as a result of poor choices and selfish motives, God's arms are open for those who will run to Him. It doesn't matter how deep the stains, God's love is extended to you.

Several years ago, I heard a story of a little girl making a pilgrimage, along with her mother, to visit her father. A job assignment in a distant state had kept the family apart for many months. The tickets were purchased and the bags were packed in great anticipation of this family reunion.

On the day of the trip, a lovely white dress outlined in lace had been chosen as the perfect attire for the little girl. They loaded the car and were quickly off to the airport.

On most flights, beverages and snacks are served as a treat for passengers. This flight proved to be no different. The little girl, in her beautiful white dress, quickly consumed her chocolate chip cookies and soda. Seeing an opportunity, she began to solicit and beg the other passengers for cookies. Before long, she had consumed many bags of chocolate chip cookies along with several cups of soda.

It was at that moment that the captain began to announce that they were expecting to encounter some turbulence and requested that all passengers wear their seat belts. As the captain had predicted, the plane began to shake violently. The atmosphere became tense and nervous. Not only did the little girl become frightened...but sick. And to make matters worse, her airsickness came on so suddenly that there was no time to retrieve the airsick bag. Needless to say, her beautiful white dress outlined in lace was now soiled.

Well, the sight of this mishap and the lingering aroma led to the fastest deplaning in the history of aviation. It also became one of the saddest moments for a little girl in a soiled white dress outlined in lace. She hadn't brought a change of clothes. She would have to meet her daddy in her soiled dress.

As she and her mom exited the plane and traveled up the concourse, she saw the silhouette of a man who looked a lot like her father holding a red rose. As she got closer, she recognized him as her daddy. She ran as fast as her little legs would take her toward the man with the red rose. He quickly knelt down and opened both arms wide to embrace his little girl. Her daddy hardly noticed the soiled dress; he only noticed how much he loved and missed his little girl. He nestled her into his arms and showered her with hugs and kisses.

That's a picture of our Heavenly Father's love for you and me. Even when our lives are soiled, His love for us is greater than our faults. Jonah experienced that same kind of love when he prayed to God inside the belly of the whale.

THE GOD OF SECOND CHANCES

Grace is all about the second chance. Hope is renewed when we discover that we have a second chance. When "The word of the Lord came to Jonah a second time" (Jon. 3:1), God was giving Jonah a second chance. In other words, Jonah was given a new beginning. The good news is that you and I can have a new beginning! Regardless of the poor choices, wrong decisions, and messes of our past, we can start again. God's grace gives us the power to close the door on yesterday's pain and failures. No failure is ever final.

Our greatest challenge, however, is to forget yesterday's pain and failures. Too many of us replay the painful memories of our past over and over in our minds. Paul says, "Forgetting what is behind and straining toward what is ahead" (Phil. 3:13b). Don't empower the painful memories of the past. Forget them and press toward the goal and purpose to which God has called you.

Shortly after I learned to drive, I was in a terrible automobile accident. My father later asked me what happened. I told him that I was looking in the rearview mirror to see if my brother was following. As I kept trying to see his car in the mirror, I hadn't noticed that a truck was stopped on the road in front of me. When I did see the truck, it was too late. I can still hear the sound of bending metal and breaking glass as I plowed into the truck's rear bumper.

I learned an important lesson that day. Don't focus on what is behind you if you want to go forward. You will have a wreck! Too many of us go through life looking in the rearview mirror. We can't seem to get our eyes off of past hurts and failures. It's as if our focus on the past will bring about a better yesterday. We need to remind ourselves that we can't change the past. God wants you to forget those things that are behind you and focus on what is ahead. And that is exactly what Jonah did when he obeyed God.

"Jonah obeyed the word of the Lord and went to Nineveh" (Jon. 3:3a). It was in obeying God that Jonah was empowered for success. God didn't need an army to fulfill His plan, He just needed one who would listen and obey. Abraham obeyed and a nation was born. Moses obeyed and a nation was delivered. Jonah obeyed and a nation was saved.

It was this same kind of obedience that caused Dr. Mordecai Ham to preach a revival in Charlotte, North Carolina, in 1934. He was a dignified, balding man with a neatly trimmed white mustache who wore round eye spectacles, but possessed the fire of a prophet. He spent weeks preparing and promoting the upcoming revival in the community. A 5,000-seat wooden tabernacle with sawdust for a floor was the chosen venue for the event.

After many nights of singing and preaching, Mordecai brought the crusade to a close. The response to the crusade was disheartening. Needless to say, the evangelist was deeply discouraged. What he didn't realize, however, was that among the few who *had* responded to Christ, was a 16-year-old teenager who just happened to be Billy Graham. If this was all that Dr. Mordecai Ham ever accomplished through obedience, then he was a success.

The Bible says, "Obey the laws of God and...you will prosper in everything you do" (1 Kings 2:3 TLB). Obedience to God brings favor and blessing. It empowers us for success. We may not always understand God's purpose or plan, but His blessing will always flow to those who are obedient.

CHAPTER 5

For Every Valley There Are Two Mountaintops

Most of us are familiar with the phrase, "a mountaintop experience." We often associate success and victory with peaks and mountains: Hillary conquering Mount Everest, and Borglum sculpting the presidents at Mount Rushmore. It's overcoming great obstacles to achieve the unthinkable. What an exhilarating feeling to stand at the top of a summit and experience a 360-degree view! Many times, however, we fail to recognize that the "mountaintop experience" is preceded by the "valley experience." For it's in the valley that God molds, equips, prepares, and strengthens us for the climb to the top of the mountain.

There is a small sapphire-blue book in my library entitled, *So Send I You.* It is written by Oswald Chambers, the man who wrote the popular *My Utmost for His Highest.* As you read through its pages, you come to a chapter entitled, "The vision, the valley, and the verity." It's here that a message is crafted and weaved revealing God's design and purpose for His people. He gives us a vision and leads us to a "valley experience" that sifts us. It's through this process that we are prepared for "greatness." It's this process of sanding, pruning, and disciplining that rids us of those hindrances that would keep us from conquering the mountain.

We discover in the Bible that battles were often fought in the valley. Joshua's greatest victory was in the Valley of Ajalon. If you remember, Joshua was running out of daylight and needed more time to defeat the

Amorites. You might say, "there were not enough hours in the day." Can you relate? So, Joshua prayed and asked God to stop the sun so that Israel could "avenge itself on its enemies" (see Josh. 10:13). And in that moment God stopped the sun and moon allowing Joshua to win the fight of a lifetime.

We also find David winning a great victory in the Valley of Salt where he utterly defeated the Philistines. It was in the Valley of Rephaim that David's soldiers heard the sound of wind in the tops of the mulberry trees, which God had promised as a sign of victory. The "valley experience" prepares us.

The fact of the matter is that people who escape trouble miss growth. The hardships of life are growing pains. Paul was made "more than a conqueror" through stripes, shipwrecks, stonings, prisons, loneliness, misunderstandings, wilderness, pain, hunger, nakedness, and weariness.

Sometimes it takes the valley of misfortune to clear our view. Our house and furnishings are destroyed. Keepsakes and valuables are burned. A lawsuit is lost. The stock market drops. A crop is ruined. A business goes under. It's here, in the valley, that many make the real finds of life. They find values that can never perish from flame or flood—values such as honor, integrity, and love. These are things that cannot be stolen.

It is in the valley, the "boot camp" of life, where climbing skills are honed and sharpened. John F. Kennedy once said, "Great crises produce great men."[26] India's former Prime Minister Nehru made an observation of the many years he spent as a political prisoner, "All my major works have been written in prison."[27] The valley experience forges men's and women's characters. It is a corridor that must be traveled, a path we must pursue to reach the summit.

In the book *The Storm and the Rainbow,* Lowell Ditzen captures the essence of the valley experience by conveying that life is made up of contrasts.

> All things in God's creation are His work—the lush meadow, and the barren desert too—the refreshing breeze and still waters, but also the destructive gales and the stormy seas. Each has its place in the total scheme, even though we may not comprehend its meaning. God does not force or drive us into the wilderness out of anger or caprice, or to punish us; but, when in the ordering of events in this

world, we are called upon to go there, we do not go alone. As He led the people of ancient Israel, so is He with us too.[28]

All of us face the ups and downs in life. We experience the good with the bad. The mountaintop experiences of life are seldom the problem. It's the valley experiences that keep us up late at night. Paul Harvey is known for saying, "In times like these it's helpful to remember that there have always been times like these." The question isn't, "Will a valley experience come?" but "How will I handle it when it does?"

LOOK TO THE FINISH LINE

When I was in high school a friend asked me to join the track team. I thought it was a great idea. I liked running and jumping, so why not? I decided to try out and run the hurdles. I had visions of competing in the Olympics, wearing the gold, hearing the national anthem, and having my picture on the Wheaties cereal box.

After crashing through most of the hurdles with the grace of a three-legged elephant, the coach called all of us into a circle. I'll never forget what he said, "You guys are obsessed with the hurdles and are taking your eyes off the finish line. Keep your eyes on the finish line and the hurdles will take care of themselves." It made a world of difference. We knocked over fewer and fewer hurdles by concentrating on the finish line. Unfortunately, I still did not make it to the Olympics or make the cover of the Wheaties cereal box.

However, that experience taught me that it is crucial that you keep your eyes on the goal. Focus is essential. Too often obstacles and hindrances can distract us from reaching the summit. Henry Ford said, "Obstacles are those frightful things you see when you take your eyes off the goal."[29] Unfortunately for many, these obstacles become insurmountable barriers. If we are going to achieve the mountaintop experience, we must tenaciously climb with purpose. Focusing on the goal helps us to overcome the obstacles we face in our climb to the summit.

In a valley experience it's easy to lose perspective. The mountain looks too high. The obstacles seem too large. The climb seems too hard. It's important to see beyond the present and look ahead. This strenuous experience is only for a season. You will not always be in the depression of a valley. Focus on when this experience will be far behind you. Keep your eyes on the summit!

LOOK TO GOD FOR STRENGTH

While visiting the lush green country of El Salvador, missionary Don Triplett challenged us to climb a nearby volcano on our free day. He said the view from the top would be spectacular and would be one of those unforgettable "once in a lifetime" experiences. We all set out as explorers on a bold and daring adventure. With our boots on, cameras around our necks, and water in our backpacks, we began.

It didn't take us long to realize that climbing a volcano of lava rock and ash was arduous work. After several hours, we were barely halfway to the summit. Because of the tremendous strain, several in our group decided to return to the base of the volcano. Although I was feeling the effects of fatigue, I continued.

When I neared the summit, my energy gave way. My feet felt like lead and my arms felt like jelly. The altitude, dehydration, and the grueling climb were taking their toll. I actually didn't think I could make it another step. I remember hearing voices from above of those who had reached the summit successfully. They were yelling to me, "You can make it! Don't give up! Just one more step…just one more step!" And so, that's what I did. I took one step at a time until I finally collapsed at the top. After a moment of rest, I experienced the panoramic view and shared in the exhilarating feeling of conquering the volcano. With the help and encouragement of others, I reached the summit.

It's important to remember that your strength is not enough. You need God's strength to help you on your quest to the summit. His strength will sustain you when you feel you can't go on. A sign on the wall of my office simply says, "It is not how troubled the sea is that determines the course of your life, it is who the pilot is." Remember, God is the pilot of your ship! He hasn't brought you this far to see you fail. Look to Him for strength in the hour of struggle. The Bible says, "Blessed is the man whose strength is in Thee" (Ps. 84:5a KJV).

When you first encounter the valley experience, you will feel overwhelmed. You will only find the stamina to endure this trial with God's help. Keep moving! Keep climbing! Don't give up! Take it one step at a time.

LOOK ON THE BRIGHT SIDE

It's important to see the value of the valley experience. The winds and waves of adversity make it difficult for us to understand their benefits. Often we are tempted to make it a place of despair, bitterness, and unforgiveness. But God is accomplishing His purpose through these trials. He is using these circumstances to mold, refine, and perfect us. Paul said, "For our light and momentary troubles are achieving for us an eternal glory that far outweighs them all" (2 Cor. 4:17). It is possible that you may have to live and work in difficult situations. You may have to endure great hardships. But understand—God is creating a masterpiece; a "work of art" with your life.

I once read a bumper sticker that said, "Never give up; you can always be used as a bad example." Though humorous, it reminds us that there is always a bright side to the challenges we face. Even when it rains—it's the rain that waters the plants and brings bounty to the harvest. We don't have to like the rain; we just have to understand its purpose. The troubles that we face ultimately work toward our good and produce fruit in our lives. God has a way of cultivating and preparing us for His eternal purpose. Many times cultivating requires adversity. Like the twisting and bending of clay by the potter to form a beautiful vase, so God fashions us into a reflection of His Son, Jesus Christ.

It also takes the valley experience to slow us down. So often we race through life clamored by relentless schedules and staggering demands. Our families become casualties of selfish pursuits and certificates of achievements. We make ourselves sick working toward a secure future only to find at the end of life we have never lived. It's in our valley experiences that we discover the true treasures in life.

Recently, a friend sent a poem to me entitled "It's in the Valleys I Grow." It illustrates how important the valley experiences are in our lives. Here are a few lines:

Sometimes life seems hard to bear,
Full of sorrow, trouble and woe
It's then I have to remember
That it's in the valleys I grow.

If I always stayed on the mountain top
And never experienced pain,
I would never appreciate God's love
And would be living in vain.

I have so much to learn
And my growth is very slow,
Sometimes I need the mountain tops,
But it's in the valleys I grow.

I do not always understand
Why things happen as they do,
But I am very sure of one thing.
My Lord will see me through.

———•—

Continue to strengthen me, Lord
And use my life each day
To share your love with others
And help them find their way.

Thank you for valleys, Lord
For this one thing I know
The mountain tops are glorious
But it's in the valleys I grow![30]

LOOK TO HELP OTHERS

Psalm 84:6a says, "As they pass through the Valley of Baca, they make it a place of springs." It's important to note that God wants to use you to help others traveling the same path. Create a spring in your "valley experience" so that others following might be refreshed. Make an oasis for the hurting.

I remember talking to my mother during one of the darkest seasons of my life. I was in need of encouragement, comfort, and solace. As she patiently listened to my "Job experience," she spoke words that jarred my soul. "I hope you never forget the pain you are feeling."

What? I couldn't believe my ears! This wasn't the comfort I was needing or seeking. It wasn't until she continued that I understood. "Someday…you will be able to relate and help someone else who is hurting the same way you are hurting."

I cannot count the many times her prophetic words have come true. As I listen to the cries of people hurting from their valley experiences, her words ring loudly. With God's help, I have been able to speak hope and encouragement to those who have trodden the misty valley of uncertainty and pain that I once traveled.

I've heard it said, "It is nice to know that when you help someone up the hill you are a little nearer the top yourself." It's in the process of helping others that our lives are slowly healed.

God said, "I will…transform her Valley of Troubles into a Door of Hope" (Hosea 2:15a TLB). In other words, God is opening a door, making a way, and creating a miracle for you in your valley of trouble. Don't stop until you see the door open. Don't quit until the path is made clear. Don't give up until a miracle is yours. Remember, God has not abandoned you! He's opening a door.

It's often in the valley of crisis that God speaks the loudest. When difficulties come you can either make a commitment to trust Him with confidence or collapse in fear. God has designed you to be a conqueror. Remember, for every valley there are two mountaintops. You will not always live in the valley experience. Soon your valley experience will be far behind you, and you will experience the summit of victory. Keep climbing!

CHAPTER 6

Healing Unfair Hurts

My wife surprised me on my birthday by buying tickets for our family to see the St. Louis Cardinals play the Atlanta Braves. The gift came complete with Twizzlers, peanuts, bubble gum, and Cardinals' hat and shirt. She thought of everything! We drove to St. Louis and experienced one of the greatest games in baseball history.

On the way back, I became very ill. I quickly pulled off the Interstate to find a convenient place to stop. Finding a department store, I parked the car and went inside. When I came back, my wife shared the play-by-play experience of "waiting in the car."

While waiting in the car, our youngest son Jonathan asked if he could go in with Daddy. My wife explained that Daddy would be out soon and they would just wait in the car until he returned. He persisted, "Mommy, I want to go in with Daddy!"

She said, "Son, Daddy is sick. He will be out soon."

Not taking no for an answer, he responded, "Mommy, I sick too!"

Realizing that our four-year-old was trying to pull a fast one on her, she asked him, "If you are sick, what part of your body is hurting?"

He thought for a moment then said, "Mommy, my feelings are hurting."

All of us know what it is like to be hurt. It is very possible that you have experienced a cutting word from a friend or a betrayal of a relative.

It may have occurred yesterday or a lifetime ago. It haunts you day and night. You did not deserve the hurt, but it lingers. Whatever the circumstance, each of us at some point has felt its sting. To some, our hurts may seem superficial and small, but they are not the ones who feel them—we do.

It seems that some people have the ability to release their hurts. Their painful moments seem to fly away on the wings of forgetfulness. Most of us, however, struggle with these unpleasant memories. We fantasize "what if" and "if only," hoping to ease our turmoil. In extreme cases we can find ourselves becoming reclusive and unproductive. Hannah Arendt, the great Jewish philosopher, found in her study on *The Human Condition* that the only power that could stop the torrent of painful memories was the "faculty of forgiveness."

There is hope for healing the hurts and wounds of our souls. Hope is a fruit produced on the tree of forgiveness. We experience freedom and healing when we forgive those who have hurt us deeply. Forgiveness is the doorway that leads to reconciliation. It promotes restoration in broken relationships. It yields hope to wounded hearts. Forgiveness allows us to heal.

THE "FACULTY OF FORGIVENESS"

Dr. Lewis Smedes, in his book *Forgive and Forget,* gives us four stages that we must go through to reach reconciliation and healing. Here is his description of the four stages:

> The first stage is *hurt:* when somebody causes you pain so deep and unfair that you cannot forget it, you are pushed into the first stage of the crisis of forgiving.

> The second stage is *hate:* you cannot shake the memory of how much you were hurt, and you cannot wish your enemy well. You sometimes want the person who hurt you to suffer as you are suffering.

> The third stage is *healing:* you are given the 'magic eyes' to see the person who hurt you in a new light. Your

memory is healed, you turn back the flow of pain and are free again.

The fourth stage is *the coming together:* you invite the person who hurt you back into your life; if he or she comes honestly, love can move you both toward a new and healed relationship. The fourth stage depends on the person you forgive as much as it depends on you; sometimes he or she doesn't come back and you have to be healed alone.[31]

WE HURT

Let's explore these four stages a little further. The first stage we encounter, which moves us into a crisis of forgiveness, is hurt. Dr. Smedes shares that this stage has three dimensions. It's personal, unfair, and always deep. This type of hurt always leads us to a crossroad of decision. We must decide whether we want to be healed or continue to suffer from this unfair assault.

If we choose the path of healing, we first must realize that we can only forgive people. We cannot forgive systems. People may feel hampered or oppressed by a political or governmental system. Others can feel trapped in poverty or lose large amounts of money through a poor economic climate. A corporate infrastructure can push people from one state to another, from one office to another or, even worse, terminate employment. But it's people we forgive—not systems.

There are several reasons. First, it is people who can be held accountable for their actions and choices. And second, only people can receive and accept forgiveness.

We also must acknowledge that we have been hurt. Some hide and deny their pain because it hurts too much to confess. Some refuse to concede that they were vulnerable enough to be wounded. Others live in fear and are afraid to admit the hurt from those they most dearly want to love. In every case, we must come to terms with the hurt and its painful memories. Dr. Smedes makes this observation, "The miracle of healing happens when one person feels the pain and forgives the person who opened the wound."[32]

WE HATE

It is a natural tendency of human nature to become bitter toward those who have hurt us unfairly—to harbor ill will toward someone who has brought us harm. Hatred can become a corrupt influence in the way we think and respond. It often poisons our attitude and robs our joy.

My father once told me, "Hate and bitterness will create a monster of you." He continued, "Son, whatever happens, don't allow hate and bitterness to dominate and control your life. You must learn to forgive."

What wise counsel my father gave. I've often reminded myself of those words when looking into the face of bitterness and hatred. It has been this influence that has helped me through some challenging moments. My father's words were the inspiration for this brief allegory entitled, "The River of Pain."

> After a horrific crisis in my life several years ago, I found myself at an emotional River of Pain. There were no bridges or rafts to guide me to the distant shore. Every attempt to make it safely to the other bank only widened the river. Before long the river was so wide that it became impossible to cross. I became frustrated and angry as I pondered the massive River of Pain.
>
> At first, the bitterness inside me made little change in my appearance and attitude. But soon I began to snarl and fume at every person, animal, and creature that came near the Path of Hate. I noticed my features began to change as my hate began to grow. Little children would scream in horror at my appearance, while adults would turn their heads in disgust. I thought to myself, "How I long to cross the River of Pain to reach the Shore of Healing."
>
> It happened by chance that an elderly man with a long white beard and bent cane passed near. In his wisdom he said, "There is a way to cross the River of Pain."
>
> I snapped back, "That's impossible! I've already searched the bank and there is no way across."

"Oh, but there is," replied the old man. "I've crossed it many times on many occasions."

With a skeptical look and in a dubious voice I responded, "How is it possible?"

Speaking empathetically he said, "The only way across is to build a Bridge of Forgiveness." And before I could ask another question, the old man disappeared.

As I considered what the elderly man with the long white beard and bent cane had said, I could imagine myself safely on the Shore of Healing. So I purposed in my heart to build a Bridge of Forgiveness. I started with the columns of "New Insight." This helped me to understand why my friend hurt me. I then added the boards of "New Feelings." This gave me the strength and ability to take steps toward the Shore of Healing. I then hammered the nails of "New Memories." This allowed me the freedom to release the person who hurt me. Before long, I had completed the Bridge of Forgiveness.

As I journeyed across the bridge, I saw my reflection in the waters of the River of Pain. With each step toward the shore, I could see my appearance was being restored. I realized I was safely on the Shore of Healing when I had the power to wish the person well who hurt me.

The old man was right. The way to cross the River of Pain is to build a Bridge of Forgiveness.

WE HEAL

As in the above allegory, we must first imagine our lives healed and whole. This is much like what we imagine before a crucial and necessary surgery. Second, we must cut out the wrong that has been done to us so that we can see our "enemy" in a new light. It's important to note that this is not just ignoring the wrong. This is simply a process by which we separate that person from the hurt and let it go, like a child releasing a balloon into the air and watching it drift out of sight. Third, we invite that person back into our memory as if the offense had never occurred. This releases the grip of pain in our memory and healing begins.

There is a test to judge whether forgiveness has begun. I have used it many times and it's this: "Forgiveness has begun when you recall those who hurt you and feel the power to wish them well."[33] Why not see if you would pass the test. If you find it difficult to wish the person well who hurt you, then true forgiveness has not yet begun.

It takes strength to forgive. Forgiveness is a choice that requires a commitment of the will. It is sometimes referred to as grace or mercy. William Ward writes, "We are most like beasts when we kill. We are most like men when we judge. We are most like God when we forgive."[34] Forgiveness is God's invention to help us heal ourselves.

Peter asked Jesus, *"'How many times shall I forgive my brother when he sins against me? Up to seven times?' Jesus answered, 'I tell you, not seven times, but seventy-seven times'"* (Matt. 18:21-22). Peter thought he was being benevolent when he suggested seven times as the number of times to forgive a person. Jesus surprises us with His response of 77 times. In other words, Jesus is saying, "Don't keep a record of the wrongs done to you."

We find this same thought in First Corinthians 13:5, "[love] keeps no record of wrongs." If we are going to be genuine people of love, a reflection of Christ, we will no longer keep score. Love is God's prescription to heal unfair hurt and it is administered as a dose of forgiveness. We find forgiveness as the remedy in this illustration:

> On a cold winter evening a man suffered a heart attack, and after being admitted to the hospital, asked the nurse to call his daughter. He explained, "You see, I live alone and she is the only family I have."
>
> The nurse went to phone the daughter. The daughter was quite upset and shouted over the phone, "You must not let him die! You see, Dad and I had a terrible argument almost a year ago. I haven't seen him since. All these months I've wanted to go to him for forgiveness. The last thing I said to him was 'I hate you.' " The daughter cried and then said, "I'm coming now—I'll be there in thirty minutes."

The patient went into cardiac arrest and "code blue" was sounded. The nurse prayed, "Oh, God, his daughter is coming. Don't let it end this way." The efforts of the medical team to revive the patient were fruitless. The nurse observed one of the doctors talking to the daughter outside the room. She could see the pathetic hurt in her face. The nurse took the daughter and said, "I'm sorry."

The daughter responded, "I never hated him, you know. I love him, and now I want to go see him."

The nurse thought, *Why put yourself through more pain?* But she took her to the room where her father lay. The daughter went to the bed and buried her face in the sheets as she said good-bye to her deceased father. The nurse, as she tried not to look at this sad good-bye, noticed a scrap of paper on the bedside table. She picked it up and read: "My dearest Janie, I forgive you. I pray you will also forgive me. I know that you love me. I love you, too. Daddy."[35]

WE UNITE (COMING TOGETHER)

Forgiveness has the potential to bring us together. It promotes fellowship and reconciliation. It allows a bridge to be built over the wrong that separates us and unites us by a common link. The differences that divided us now become a bond to strengthen us. It allows healthy community and communication in a relationship that was once divided.

A story is told of two unmarried sisters who had so bitter a ruckus they stopped speaking to each other. Unable or unwilling to separate, the pair lived in a large single room with two beds. A chalk line divided the sleeping area into two halves, separating doorway and fireplace, so that each could come and go and get her own meals without trespassing on her sister's domain. In the black of night each could hear the breathing of the foe. For years they coexisted in spiteful silence. Neither was willing to take the first step to reconciliation.[36]

Does this story sound familiar? Has something ever happened in your life to polarize a relationship, a friendship, or a family member? Someone hurt you deeply; it was unwarranted, unjust, inexcusable, and reprehensible. This is probably no comfort, but all of us have experienced the same. Life is filled with unfair assaults. Too often we live a life of absurdity as a result of being wronged. We get the invisible chalk and start drawing lines and boundaries to cut people out of our lives. And yet, we find little solace or comfort in writing off a once close relationship. Reconciliation can only happen when we forgive.

We must also understand that there are occasions when reconciliation is not possible. For example, the person who hurt you is now deceased. In this case, we are not given the opportunity to reunite or "come together." It is important to realize that healing can still take place, even when reconciliation will not happen. Our lives can still feel the release of a painful hurt.

Forgiving is a very personal action. No one can be forced to forgive. It can only happen as a result of our choice. Forgiving is a process of the heart. It is a silent resolve to act benevolently toward a person who caused us harm. It is a reflection of the very nature of Christ. The Bible says, "Forgive as the Lord forgave you" (Col. 3:13b). When we forgive, we mirror God's love toward us. We become an extension of His grace and mercy.

Forgiving is for our benefit. When we forgive, a process of healing begins in our heart. It acts as a salve or antibiotic to the festering wound. In essence, when we forgive others, we heal ourselves. We release all the undeserved, unfair hurts bottled up deep in our lives. It's not ignoring the hurt. It's feeling the hurt and choosing to release its hold on our lives. We are able to enjoy life again. Our joy is restored. Our attitude is renewed.

We are healed.

CHAPTER 7

Why We Have Hope

I remember hearing many years ago of a train traveling through the night in a violent storm. The lightning cracked fiercely as the heavy rains pelted the passenger car windows. The wind gusts rattled the train causing it to sway as the waters began to rise toward the tracks. Minutes seemed like hours as the storm continued to overwhelm and terrorize the passengers.

In the midst of the commotion one little boy seemed to be at perfect peace. His unusually calm demeanor during such a frantic time amazed the passengers. Finally one man asked, "How is it that you can be so calm when all the rest of us are so worried."

The little boy smiled and responded, "My father is the engineer."

The young boy experienced calm in the storm because of his relationship with his father. You and I can experience the same kind of calm in the storms of life because of our relationship to our Heavenly Father. We have hope because God loves us. Through the good and bad times of life, His love for us never changes. His love never stops, never quits, never dies, never depletes, and, most of all, never fails.

God's love liberates us from fear. It breathes hope and life into the most challenging of moments. We read in First John 4:18a, "There is no fear in love. But perfect love drives out fear." Love promotes trust and confidence. We no longer fear the future because we trust that God is working all things out for our good. Our hearts are comforted because God cares for us.

GOD IS WITH US

Upon returning home from a soccer game with my youngest son, we noticed a car parked in front of our house. As we piled out of our van, the young couple that was in the car got out and approached us. They smiled graciously, extended a cordial greeting, and then asked, "Did you experience fear as a result of the September 11th tragedy?"

It caused me to pause for a moment to consider how the tragedy had affected me. Although I was grieved at the tragic loss of life, I was not taken hostage by the grip of fear. I explained that Jesus Christ was the Shepherd of my life. My past, present, and future were in His hands. It was because of His abiding love that I was not overwhelmed by fear.

The 23rd Psalm gives us an active ingredient that liberates the believer from fear. Psalm 23:4 says this, "Even though I walk through the valley of the shadow of death, I will fear no evil, for You are with me; Your rod and Your staff, they comfort me."

The Bible reinforces this thought in Isaiah when God says, "Do not fear, for I am with you; do not be dismayed, for I am your God. I will strengthen you and help you; I will uphold you with my righteous right hand" (Isa. 41:10). The awareness that God is with us frees us from fear. His presence gives us a sense of assurance that all is well—much like a frightened child who finds comfort and solace in the arms of a parent.

During the Christmas season, many of us enjoy hearing and singing Christmas carols about the birth of Christ. Many of these beloved songs refer to Baby Jesus as "Immanuel," which is taken from the Gospels. The very word *Immanuel* means "God with us." God conveys this message of comfort to you and me in the very name of His Son.

Interesting enough, Jesus' last words before His ascension was, "And surely I am with you always, to the very end of the age" (Matt. 28:20b). Throughout the Bible, God has threaded the message that He is with us. He never slumbers nor sleeps but is a loving Heavenly Father who constantly is watching over us. We experience immunity from fear as we cling to the Creator who is constantly abiding. Confidence in His promise that He will never leave us nor forsake us (see Heb. 13:5) is the foundation of comfort.

GOD IS FOR US

Each of us, at some point, has ridden into battle with the express purpose of conquering our ageless foe named "fear." Did you know that Thomas Edison, the inventor of the light bulb, was afraid of the dark? Julius Caesar, the mighty conqueror and Roman emperor, feared thunder. Fear, whether real or imagined, is still fear. It is an adversary that haunts our mind and challenges our will. Many a brave soul has encountered the fury of this emotion of monstrous proportions. In 1623, Sir Francis Bacon said, "Nothing is terrible except for fear itself." Then 200 years later the Duke of Wellington declared, "The only thing I am afraid of is fear." And most of us recognize the assertion from our beloved President Franklin D. Roosevelt who said, "The only thing we have to fear is fear itself."[37]

Most of the fears we combat daily are a result of feelings. Have you any idea how much it is costing you to fear things that never happen? Legitimate concerns based on fact are rarely the focus. For example, a study at the University of Michigan revealed the following:

- 60 percent of our fears are totally unwarranted; they never come to pass.

- 20 percent of our fears are focused on our past, which is completely out of our control.

- 10 percent of our fears are based on things so petty that they make no difference in our lives.

- Of the remaining 10 percent, only 4 to 5 percent could be considered justifiable.[38]

If the above statistics are correct, then 95 percent of the time we worry and fret over nothing!

John Maxwell shares a humorous story about fear to which some of us can relate: There was a couple in bed late one night…

> The husband was sound asleep until his wife jabbed him in the ribs, saying, "Burt, wake up. I hear a burglar downstairs. Burt, wake up!"
>
> "Okay, okay," said Burt as he sat up on the edge of the bed and searched for his slippers for what seemed like the

ten-thousandth time. "I'm up." He grabbed his robe and stumbled groggily out into the hall and down the stairs. When he reached the bottom step, he found himself staring into the barrel of a gun.

"Hold it right there, buddy," a voice said firmly from behind a ski mask. "Show me where the valuables are."

Burt did. When the burglar had his bag full and was getting ready to leave, Burt said, "Wait. Before you go, could you go up and meet my wife? She's been expecting you every night for more than thirty years."[39]

Fear is the absence of faith. It robs us of God's power to do the impossible. The Bible says, "Without faith it is impossible to please God" (Heb. 11:6a). This is a significant statement in God's Word, revealing the importance of faith in the eyes of God. You see, God attributes great value to the everyday operation of faith in our lives. It is faith that touches His heart and moves Him into action. It is this blind trust wrapped in a blanket of hope that causes the miraculous.

I've been told that "fear not" is mentioned 365 times in the Bible. That's a "fear not" for each day of the year. Although I have not taken time to count them, I have noticed that this phrase is mentioned often. It is a phrase that promotes faith. It draws our attention back to God and allows us to focus on His abilities. In essence, when we display fear we are saying, "God, I don't trust You." Our view is prejudiced by our limitations. We only see God through the eyes of our weakness and inability. Faith, on the other hand, sees beyond the impossible to the possible. It's living with the preoccupation of His ability rather than our inadequacy. It sees God larger than life.

Isaiah certainly saw God larger than life! His writing rocks the scales as his words paint the grandeur of God. Isaiah's perspective of God is breathtaking:

> *Who has measured the waters in the hollow of His hand, or with the breadth of His hand marked off the heavens? Who has held the dust of the earth in a basket, or weighed the mountains on the scales and the hills in a balance? Who has understood the mind of the Lord, or*

instructed Him as His counselor? Whom did the Lord consult to enlighten Him, and who taught Him the right way? Who was it that taught Him knowledge or showed Him the path of understanding?...To whom then will you compare God?...Do you not know? Have you not heard? Has it not been told you from the beginning? Have you not understood since the earth was founded? He sits enthroned above the circle of the earth, and its people are like grasshoppers. He stretches out the heavens like a canopy, and spreads them out like a tent to live in. He brings princes to naught and reduces the rulers of this world to nothing.... "To whom will you compare Me? Or who is My equal?" says the Holy One. Lift your eyes and look to the heavens: Who created all these? He who brings out the starry host one by one, and calls them each by name. Because of His great power and mighty strength, not one of them is missing. ...Do you not know? Have you not heard? The Lord is the everlasting God, the Creator of the ends of the earth. He will not grow tired or weary, and His understanding no one can fathom (Isaiah 40:12-14, 18, 21-23, 25-26, 28).

Life is made up of choices. Every day you and I must decide whether we will feed faith or feed fear. If we feed faith, it will grow. If we feed fear, it will grow. The one we feed the most will be the one that dominates our life. Which one are you feeding? If we would feed our faith with God's Word, our fears would starve to death. Are you a man or woman of faith or of fear? God encourages us to "fear not."

GOD LOVES US

Did you know that God is thinking of you? Right now—this very moment—God, the Creator of the universe, is thinking of you. Has it ever crossed your mind that you are on His mind? If God were to send you a card, it would probably say something like: "I can't get you off of My mind" or "Just thinking of you!" We recognize these phrases as a sentiment from the heart, a term of endearment, and an expression of intimacy. Greeting card companies have made a fortune by capturing these expressions. We often say to our loved ones when we depart, "I'll think of you every day." It makes the sting of separation tolerable when we bathe our minds with loving memories. The Psalmist has written, "How precious also are Your thoughts to me, O God! How great is the sum of them! If I should count them, they would be more in number than the sand; when I awake, I am still with You" (Ps. 139:17-18 NKJV).

You are always on God's mind. His full attention is always devoted to you. His thoughts of you outnumber the sands of the sea and the salt of the ocean! There is never a time or place that you escape His view. He contemplates ways to reveal His love to you while attending to your every need. He refers to you as His friend and takes great care to watch over you. In fact, He is crazy about you! If God had a wallet, your photo would be inside. If God had a refrigerator, your picture would be on it. He notices your every joy, pain, sorrow, and tear. Your name has been engraved in the palm of His hand. The Bible even says that He sings about you. "He will take great delight in you, He will quiet you with His love, He will rejoice over you with singing" (Zeph. 3:17b). You may ask, "Why would God be so preoccupied with me?" Because He loves you!

The Bible expresses in many ways God's love for you. The heart of God longs and yearns for you. You are not simply a name or number. You are not part of some cosmic game or puzzle. But God loves you deeply! So much that He sent His only Son to die for you. The Bible says, "But God demonstrates His own love for us in this: While we were still sinners, Christ died for us" (Rom. 5:8). The Bible reiterates this in First John 4:10: "This is love: not that we loved God, but that He loved us and sent His Son as an atoning sacrifice for our sins."

It's important to note that God is pursuing you! He is passionate about you! He is consumed and preoccupied with thoughts of you! He was on the cross dying to know you! He rose from the grave to find you! God loves you!

This true story illustrates the kind of love God has for you. A little boy had a sister who needed a blood transfusion...

> The doctor explained that she had the same disease the boy had recovered from two years earlier. Her only chance of recovery was a transfusion from someone who had previously conquered the disease. Since the

two children had the same rare blood type, the boy was an ideal donor.

"Would you give your blood to Mary?" the doctor asked.

Johnny hesitated. His lower lip started to tremble. Then he smiled and said, "Sure, for my sister."

Soon the two children were wheeled into the hospital room. Mary, pale and thin. Johnny, robust and healthy. Neither spoke, but when their eyes met, Johnny grinned.

As the nurse inserted the needle into his arm, Johnny's smile faded. He watched the blood flow through the tube.

With the ordeal almost over, Johnny's voice, slightly shaky, broke the silence.

"Doctor, *when do I die?*"

"Only then did the doctor realize why Johnny had hesitated, why his lip had trembled when he agreed to donate his blood. He thought giving his blood to his sister would mean giving up his life.[40]

Have you ever taken into consideration the breadth of God's love? His love far surpasses the love of a father, mother, spouse, or child. It's this kind of love that casts out all fear and brings comfort to our lives.

GOD COMFORTS US

I have a friend who is a pastor of a large church in the Midwest. His name is Pastor Comfort. I've always admired his ministry and his name. In my opinion, it is the perfect name for a pastor. Why? Because we live in a world filled with hurting people. It's a world where grief and despair perpetuate the landscape. The number of violent crimes—murders, rapes, robberies, and aggravated assaults—has increased 550 percent during the last four decades.[41] Suicide among teenagers is up 200 percent over the same period.[42] According to the Bureau of Justice Statistics, 645,400 juveniles were arrested in 1999 for violent and property crimes; 38 percent of those were under the age of 15.[43] We live in a world abundant in wickedness and pain. It's a world where hurting people are desperate for relief and need to be comforted.

When we think of the word *comfort,* our minds generate a rainbow of images. The word *comfort* actually comes from the Latin word *confortare,* which means, "to strengthen much." Its meaning over the years has broadened to include: to give hope, to cheer, to gladden, to relieve distress, to allay trouble, to console. It's with this in mind that we can understand how God is the God of all comfort.

God does not insulate us from our struggles, but rather is a loving, consoling Father who meets us in the midst of our troubles. We read in Second Corinthians 1:3-4,

> *Praise be to the God and Father of our Lord Jesus Christ, the Father of compassion and the God of all comfort, who comforts us in all our troubles, so that we can comfort those in any trouble with the comfort we ourselves have received from God.*

Paul continues in verses 8-9 by saying,

> *We do not want you to be uninformed, brothers, about the hardships we suffered in the province of Asia. We were under great pressure, far beyond our ability to endure, so that we despaired even of life. Indeed, in our hearts we felt the sentence of death. But this happened that we might not rely on ourselves but on God...*

Maybe you can relate to Paul. You may feel like a number one failure. It seems you can't do anything right. You realize the "train of success" has just passed by and you were not a passenger. Your family seems to be falling apart, your job is going nowhere, and it's hard to keep your head above water. You may be experiencing pressure so great that it seems impossible to endure—even to the point of despair!

If you can relate, then you are the kind of person God is looking for: a person who knows that when good things happen, it is a result of God! Christians who plow over people with their abilities and talents have never impressed God. God is looking for people who will rely on Him—who have freed themselves of distractions and hindrances to His divine purpose. He is looking for those who have emptied themselves of self and are consecrated to Him. It's an empty vessel that God seeks and chooses to fill. He desires to work through people who are filled with His power, strength, and anointing. It's this process of emptying self that makes room for God's power and allows the miraculous to happen.

If you have ever been a conduit of God's power, then you understand why Paul said, "But this happened that we might not rely on ourselves *but on God"* *(2 C*or. 1:9). You see, there's no healing for the hurting, lonely, and desperate—but God. There's no turning point for human depravity—but God. There's no deliverance from addiction and heartache—but God. There's no solution to war, prejudice, and injustice—but God. There's nothing that can fill the emptiness of the human heart—but God. It is not our talents or strength. It's not our creativity or ability. It is the power of God flowing through ordinary people to accomplish extraordinary results.

GOD CHOOSES US

God has always done more with less than men thought adequate. It seems to be a pattern with God. He chooses the most unlikely to accomplish the unthinkable with the least amount of resources. Think about it! God chose a young shepherd boy named David to defeat a towering giant—with a slingshot! He chose Moses, a man who stuttered, to speak for an enslaved nation and ultimately to lead them to freedom. God chose a beautiful woman named Esther to thwart an evil plot and influence a king to save the nation of Israel. He chose Joseph, who was sold into slavery and later became Pharaoh's second in command, to spare God's people from famine and desolation. God's choices may seem unimpressive, but they are great—not by a criteria that we might use to determine greatness, but by God's set of values. God chooses the mundane, common, and ordinary to accomplish His supernatural purpose and will.

Elijah was a man who was able to accomplish unbelievable things for God. He raised the dead, prophesied of impending famine, and prayed fire down from heaven. What a resumé! And yet, the Bible says, Elijah was "a man subject to like passions as we are" (James 5:17a KJV). He was a man who hurt like you and I hurt. He felt pain like you and I feel pain. He experienced problems just like you and I experience problems. In all of his challenges, Elijah was found to be a man who did the impossible by trusting God. He was a simple man—a nobody that God made into a somebody.

In a letter to the Corinthians, Paul wrote:

> *Not many of you were wise by human standards; not many were influential; not many were of noble birth. But God chose the foolish things of the world to shame the wise; God chose the weak things of the world to shame the strong. He chose the lowly things of this world and the despised things—and the things that are not—to nullify the things that are, so that no one may boast before Him* (1 Corinthians 1:26b-29).

I like how the New Berkeley Version expresses the translation of the last two verses, *"God also has chosen the world's insignificant and despised people and nobodies in order to bring to nothing those who amount to something, so that nobody may boast in the presence of God"* (1 Cor. 1:28-29 NBV).

Wow! What a contrast to our approach of recruiting! We will spare no expense when it comes to finding the best and the brightest. We will examine every credential and qualification. We will follow every lead and reference in our hunt for the perfect person. Our heroes and role models consist of the most beautiful, brilliant, and successful people on our planet. We research and seek the advice of the world's most famous and auspicious people of any nation. We admire the superficial and are enamored by the surface. We will cast our lot for the candidate who looks and speaks the best on television. We may not like to admit it, but we are mesmerized by the glitz and glamour of the successful. Its hypnotic lure often leads us to a prejudicial conclusion about the worth of a person.

But God's choices are gauged on a completely different standard. He looks at the heart. When God chose David to be king, the prophet Samuel said: "The Lord has sought out a man after His own heart" (1 Sam. 13:14b). In other words, God looks beyond the surface and observes the inner person. He is not betrayed by the superficial. He sees what cannot be seen with human eyes. He chooses a person who seems to us to be a "nobody" and He makes a "somebody."

Jesus said to His disciples, "You did not choose Me, but I chose you and appointed you to go and bear fruit" (John 15:16a). Just think, He chose you! There is something wonderful about being chosen. When I was a young boy, I loved to play baseball. Our neighborhood was filled with children who also loved to play baseball. We would often ride our bikes through the woods on dusty trails to reach the nearest ball diamond. With our bats and gloves, we would climb the locked fence and scramble on the field. It would be the highlight of our day to compete in the daily neighborhood "World Series." We would appoint two captains to choose teams. If anyone had a coin, we would flip it to see which captain would choose first. I can still remember the feeling of being chosen, especially if I was the first one picked.

God has chosen us! Why? The answer is simple...to be fruitful. The word *fruitful* means "to produce in abundance that which is profitable." God wants you and me to be fruitful and productive. He wants you to live a life of significance. God wants you to be successful in your marriage, family, business, and church. He has a wonderful work and future prepared for you. The Bible says, "We are God's workmanship, created in Christ Jesus to do good works, which God prepared in advance for us to do" (Eph. 2:10). The word *workmanship* means "work of art"! We are God's creation—His "work of art" created to do good works. Notice, "which God prepared in *advance* for us to do." God has a plan, purpose, mission, design, dream, expectation, destination, and direction for your life. He always has! He always will! It is a plan that He has ordained in advance. God has a good work—and He's chosen you for the task!

Could it be that you've argued with God? Have you resigned yourself to the fact that you have nothing to offer? Do you struggle with a sense of being inadequate? Are you disturbed by the thought that there is no purpose for your life? Then you are a candidate for God's blessing. It might just be that you are the one for whom God is looking. Perhaps you are the one that God is choosing to accomplish great things. Perhaps you are God's choice to make an impact in our world. Perhaps!

CHAPTER 8

Storm Watch

Have you ever had a bad day? "One of those days" where nothing seems to go right? I have! It's been said, "You know it's going to be a bad day when your twin sister forgets your birthday. You really know it's going to be a bad day when your horn sticks while following a group of Hell's Angels." All of us, at one time or another, have experienced bad days. I recently heard a story that depicts what we would call a bad day.

Chippie the parakeet certainly had a bad day! While resting peacefully in his golden wire cage, the unexpected happened. He was sucked into a vacuum cleaner.

This whole episode began when Chippie's owner decided to clean the cage. She carefully removed the vacuum head and stuck the hose into the cage. This ambitious effort was suddenly interrupted by the ring of the telephone. As she turned to answer the phone, she heard "sssopp!" The vacuum had just swallowed Chippie the parakeet.

Chippie's owner immediately dropped the phone, turned off the vacuum, and hurriedly opened the latch to free the bird from its dusty sarcophagus. The alacritous effort of the owner prevailed. There was Chippie—still alive, but dazed and dirty.

Since the bird was coated with dust and painted with soot, she raced him to the bathroom, turned on the faucet, and held Chippie under the frigid running water. Then, realizing the shaken and shivering state of her pet, she did what any compassionate bird lover would do…she grabbed the hair dryer, took aim, and blasted him with hot air.

Chippie was never quite the same after this unexpected ordeal. A reporter from the local newspaper called to inquire of Chippie's condition. The owner replied, "Well, Chippie doesn't sing much anymore—he just sits and stares."

I think most of us can relate to this story. One minute things are going fine until all of a sudden, the unexpected storms of life come crashing in. You are sucked in, washed up, and blown away. Life is filled with unforeseen, startling, and sudden surprises. You arrive to work only to be handed a pink slip. You hear the doctor say, "It's malignant." The officer at your door says, "There's been an accident." You're handed a registered letter that reads, "We'll see you in court." The voice on the phone says, "I'm sorry to tell you this." Your minister says, "You'd better sit down."

The wind of adversity comes upon us suddenly! Its fury challenges our faith and dampens our hope. Its shock can send us spiraling into moments of depression. Our minds are assailed by waves of questions. Our hearts hear the howling winds of doubt. We seek shelter from the persistent rains of anxiety. Our lives that were so calm are now so stormy.

Jesus is aware of the storm. He knows our struggle. Yet, why doesn't He do something? Does that sound familiar?

THE STORM

If it weren't for the occasional breeze from the lake, the heat would be unbearable. The sound of water lapping on shore fuels the thirst of the disciples. These men are exhausted! After all, they have just finished serving a meal of fish and bread to 5,000 people in the blistering sun. There is no hesitation or delay, no arguing or complaining, when Jesus tells them to get in the boat and row to the other side (see Matt. 14:22). Retreating from the crowd and getting some much-needed rest seems just what the doctor ordered. The only obstacle at this point is the lake. But how tough would that be for seasoned fishermen?

As the disciples embark upon their journey to the other shore, trouble seems to follow. Suddenly, and without warning, a storm descends upon the tiny vessel. Dark clouds billow high into the heavens as bolts of lightning crack the sky and thunder shakes the earth. The once calm Sea of Galilee becomes a mountain range of white-capped waves of eerie green. The disciples are pelted by relentless waves and high winds. Their faces sting with every caustic slap of water. The occasional immersion by rogue waves leaves the men wet and weary as they cling to their craft. Every effort seems fruitless as they are swallowed into the night.

WHERE IS JESUS?

But where is Jesus? Did He not compel them to get in the boat and go to the other side? Were they not following His command? Certainly, they are not out of God's will! So, where is Jesus?

Here's a thought that may raise a few eyebrows. Storms come upon us, even when we are in the center of God's will. In other words, doing what God has called you to do will not make you immune to the troubles of life. Notice, "Jesus made the disciples get into the boat and go on ahead of Him to the other side" (Matt. 14:22). The King James Version says, "Jesus constrained His disciples to get into a ship." The word *constrained* means "to necessitate." In other words, it was absolutely necessary for the disciples to get into the boat. It was imperative! Jesus had a specific purpose and plan in compelling the disciples into the ship. Would they recognize Him in the storm?

Up until this point, they recognized Jesus as a miracle worker. After all, He had just turned a few fishes and loaves of bread into a feast to feed 5,000 people. They knew Him as a great healer. They recognized Him as the friend of sinners. They saw Him when He raised the dead and opened blinded eyes. They were amazed when demons came shrieking out of the possessed simply at His command. They knew Him as a teacher who taught them to pray and forgive. But, would they recognize Jesus in the storm?

Unfortunately, the disciples who knew Jesus best could not recognize Him when the storm suddenly hit.

That really is the problem many of us face today. We can trust Jesus for healing and miracles. We can believe Him for forgiveness and salvation. We look to Him as the supplier of our every need. But, let a storm hit and our vision of Jesus becomes fuzzy. When the winds of adversity assail us and the bottom drops out, we find it difficult to see Jesus anywhere near. We refuse to believe that He would allow us to confront such a ferocious storm. Yet, though it's hard to understand, He uses the storm to teach us to trust.

During the fourth watch of the night Jesus went out to them, walking on the lake. When the disciples saw Him walking on the lake, they were terrified. "It's a ghost," they said, and cried out in fear (Matthew 14:25-26).

THE GHOST

It is in the waters of danger that man's imagination overwhelms his sense of reason. It is sailing these straits that the specter of peril and the ghost of uncertainty are summoned. It is here among the marshes that our eyes and ears deceive us. Our senses are intensified as the night is combed for glimmers of hope.

As the disciples cling to their boat amid the blurring sheets of rain, they see a faint glow in the distance. Between the lightning flashes, a silhouette appears to be gliding toward them. The fear of the sea was now being overshadowed by a new terror. A horrifying crack of a thunderbolt causes a new wave of panic. What was this apparition? "A ghost!" screams one of the disciples. Desperate thoughts race through their minds as the phantom draws near. Several hide their faces while others turn their heads.

A voice of comfort and promise is heard at the boat's edge. "Take courage! It is I! Don't be afraid." Through the storm comes the familiar voice of a friend. It is not a ghost or apparition. It is Jesus! Jesus came in a way that was totally unpredictable and unexpected. While their minds saw Jesus on the shore, distant from their treacherous struggle, Jesus was actually walking on the water to their rescue. Jesus negotiates the wind and waves and crosses the great expanse of water to attend their need. He accomplishes the unbelievable and miraculous with each step. He treads upon what we often fear the most. Jesus is greater than our problems, circumstances, and storms.

When the night is the blackest and the storm is the angriest, Jesus draws near. When the waves are the fiercest and the wind the loudest, Jesus draws near. When fear is uncontrollable and hopelessness is overwhelming, Jesus draws near. Jesus always comes near to us in the storms and troubles of life. But, do we see Him? Are we aware that He is coming to our rescue? Do we recognize Him walking on the water in the midst of the storm?

It's in the storm that we learn to know the saving, keeping, and preserving power of Christ. When educators want to teach us, they use chalkboards and graphs. When Jesus wants to teach us, He uses storms and adversity. It's in such a setting that we learn to completely rest and trust in His power. It's here that we discern His presence, whether in the middle of a miracle or the middle of a storm. How quickly we can lose our sense of His presence and feel we are left to battle the storms alone. We can feel forsaken and abandoned if we do not learn to recognize Christ in the storms of life.

THE FIRST STEP IS A DOOZY

Peter, upon recognizing Jesus, said, "Lord, if it's You, tell me to come to You on the water" (Matt. 14:28).

Jesus replied by saying, "Come."

> *Then Peter got down out of the boat, walked on the water and came toward Jesus. But when he saw the wind, he was afraid and, beginning to sink, cried out, "Lord, save me!" Immediately Jesus reached out His hand and caught Him. "You of little faith," He said, "why did you doubt?" And when they climbed into the boat, the wind died down* (Matthew 14:29-32).

Great men of faith are made from great crises. The storms of life often yield great acts of faith from desperate men. Peter was no exception.

Max Lucado writes:

> It wasn't logic that caused Moses to raise his staff on the bank of the Red Sea.
>
> It wasn't medical research that convinced Naaman to dip seven times in the river.
>
> It wasn't common sense that caused Paul to abandon the law and embrace grace.
>
> And it wasn't a confident committee that prayed in a small room in Jerusalem for Peter's release from prison. It was a fearful, desperate, band of backed-into-a-corner believers. It was a church with no options. A congregation of have-nots pleading for help.[44]

Peter, a man of extremes, was desperate! He had struggled most of the night fighting the elements. The voice of Jesus brought a response. The mere word *Come* caused him to leap out of the boat and onto the water. It wasn't until he had taken a few steps that reality struck. He was actually walking on water. How was it possible? How could this be? Then the Bible records, "But when he saw the wind, he was afraid" (Matt. 14:30a).

What a phrase! How is it possible to see the wind? And yet, it was seeing what couldn't be seen that caused Peter to fear. Isn't it interesting how something we can't see distracts us from Christ. We notice the effects it is having on our surroundings. It is creating havoc in our lives. Our world becomes a nightmare of chaos. We find ourselves saying things like, "How could this happen?" "Why did this happen?" or "What was that all about?" If only we could put our finger on this unseen menace. If only we could stop the wind. Soon the fear of what *may* happen overtakes our faith in Christ.

Such is the case with Peter. The wind and the waves distract him from the Savior. His fear of what may happen takes over. And into the tumultuous sea he slips.

"Lord save me!" cries Peter.

At that very moment, Jesus reaches out and catches him. " 'You of little faith,' He said, 'Why did you doubt?' And when they climbed into the boat, the wind died down (Matt. 14:31-32).

It is important to know who is in your boat. The company you keep does make a difference. Is Jesus in your boat? Is He a passenger? Or is He some distant ghost?

PEACE IN THE MIDST OF THE STORM

Let the storms of life drive you to God. By going to God during a season of trouble, you will discover more about who He is and who He has created you to be. If you let your storms drive you to God, you will learn what is important to God. Your faith will grow and your character will be built. It's in the storm that the steel of greatness is forged. We are fashioned and molded into the precious image of God. Like new chrome on a car, we reflect the very nature and essence of the Creator.

To have peace in the midst of the storm requires action on our part. It requires that we make a choice to turn to the Lord and ask for help. As Peter cried, "Lord save me," so must we call on the Lord. We must pursue God for His divine intervention.

When blind Bartimaeus cried out, "Jesus, Son of David, have mercy on me" (Mark 10:47), there were many who told him to be quiet. Can you relate? Have you ever been in a place in your life when you needed God to do something big—a place where only a miracle would do? Have you ever sought God with a bold petition only to hear the discouraging words of those around you who suggest that God will not hear your prayer?

Listen, we live in a world filled with faithless people who will make every effort to put God in a box. Their perspective of God is small and powerless. They pelt the believer with why God can't and why God won't. They can even be quite pious in their discourse. Yet, it often amazes me to watch God trample and crush the boxes designed to contain Him.

After such a rebuke from the crowd, blind Bartimaeus determined not to take no for an answer. The Bible records that "he shouted all the more, 'Son of David, have mercy on me!' " And at that moment, "Jesus stopped" (see Mark 10:48-49). The entire processional is halted at the tenacious plea of a blind man. So often we feel that Jesus is too busy to address our need. Other times we feel that we aren't good enough. Many times we feel we haven't achieved the right criteria to receive a miracle from the Lord. The truth of the matter is that Jesus will respond if we ask. There is no prerequisite or magic formula for a miracle. Today, Jesus will pause to meet our need if we ask.

Before Jesus touched blind Bartimaeus, He asked a question, "What do you want Me to do for you?" (Mark 10:51) I've often wondered why Jesus would ask such a question of blind Bartimaeus. It would seem rather obvious. However, Jesus wanted blind Bartimaeus to recognize his need. We must come to terms with the fact that we need help. How many of us go through life carrying emotional baggage pretending it's not there? We hurt privately. We hide our pain. We may act as if our world is one big party, when deep down inside we are dying. Our lives are filled with fear as the storm clouds accumulate.

To have peace in the midst of the storm, we must deal with our fear and recognize our need for help. We need something that will anchor our life so that no matter what happens, we won't be blown off course. God is the anchor!

He is our source of strength and our shield in time of need. This is why it is important to develop a relationship with God. To do that, we need to come sincerely and honestly to God and accept what He has done for us—that He sent Jesus Christ to earth to die in our place and to be the sacrifice for our sins.

If we have never trusted Jesus as Savior, then our biggest problem is a sin problem. It is a problem of unbelief. When we don't trust God in the storms of life, we have no one to trust. This causes fear. We cannot truly experience peace in our life until we are secure in our relationship with the Lord.

Nothing but Jesus will calm our storms and quiet our seas. Nothing but His great love will keep us as we experience difficulty, hardship, and trials. We can blame circumstances and blame other people, but until Jesus is at the center of our heart, our lives will be enslaved to fear.

God is the unmovable anchor that holds us through the roughest storms. He is the unshakable rock by which we stand. Even if we should move away from God, He never moves away from us. If we should reject Jesus, He never rejects us. That's why He is our anchor in times of storms.

When facing a storm, it's comforting to know that we are not alone. The apostle Paul was comforted in knowing that God would be with him through a ferocious storm and crushing shipwreck. He said, "Last night an angel of the God whose I am and whom I serve stood beside me and said, 'Do not be afraid…God has graciously given you the lives of all who sail with you.' So keep up your courage, men, for I have faith in God…" (Acts 27:23-25). With God by our side, there's not a storm big enough or strong enough to defeat us.

Right now would be a good time to pause and ask God for help. God will move heaven and earth to meet your need if you ask. Why not ask God to calm your storm or calm you as you pass through the storm. Why not ask God to release the burden and heaviness from your current circumstances. Ask God for wisdom in the steps you should take that would please Him and be in accordance with His Word. Ask the Lord to free you from the bondage of fear. And as you ask, trust Him to be faithful to His Word.

You alone cannot stop the sudden storms of life. But you can take the first step toward peace by saying to the Lord, "I am trusting You to help me face the challenging circumstances of life and to help me have the courage to walk through life without fear and anxiety. I trust You to walk with me and guide me through the storm safely. Your plan is to bless me not harm me, to give me a hope and a future." Remember, this storm will pass.

CHAPTER 9

For Better or Worse

It was the perfect Christmas setting: The fire in the fireplace was crackling, gifts under a perfectly decorated Christmas tree were calling out my name, and the hot apple cider on the stove was filling the room with the wonderful aroma of Christmas. What could go wrong? Well, to our amazement, a friendly spat between my brother and his wife erupted. Noticing that much of the family had paused to hear such a clatter, my brother responded to his wife, "I wear the pants in the family!" At which his wife quickly answered, "Yes, but I'm the belt that holds up those pants in the family."

Does that sound familiar? Can you identify? I've heard it said that Adam and Eve had the ideal marriage. He didn't have to hear about all the men she could have married, and she didn't have to hear about the way his mother cooked. Marriage can sometimes be a pressure cooker. Our differences can cause us to stew over the smallest things.

Billy Graham was recently interviewed on *Oprah*. When asked what he was most thankful for, he said, "Salvation given to us in Jesus Christ," then added, "and the way you have made people all over this country aware of the power of being grateful."

When asked his secret of love, being married 54 years to the same person, Billy Graham said, "Ruth and I are happily incompatible." What an eye-opening response, certainly something to consider. Each of us could temper the challenges of marriage if we would find the strength in being grateful and happily incompatible.

It's with this in mind that we approach the subject of marriage. A great deal of hopelessness has been experienced by thousands of married couples in this world. They often feel locked in what appears to be a miserable marriage created by years of neglect and abuse.

To be honest, it would take several volumes to address the multitude of challenges and needs facing married couples. This chapter is not designed to address specifics, but to offer hope. Every marriage, regardless of the circumstances, has hope. The Bible gives us this promise that "with God all things are possible" (Matt. 19:26b). If both husband and wife are willing to trust God and take the necessary steps to heal their relationship, they will experience a rewarding marriage. "Irreconcilable differences" is not a part of God's vocabulary. It's not a part of His divine nature. He is the "Great Counselor" who desires to see you fulfilled and happy in a marriage that glorifies Him.

A WONDERFUL INVENTION

Marriage is God's idea. It's His design and creation. From the beginning, God purposed that man and woman would mutually benefit from sharing in a loving relationship. Marriage precedes all other institutions including the church. God, recognizing man's deep need for companionship and observing that all the other creatures of the field had a companion, set forth to complete His work of creation. With a stroke of genius and artistry, God wonderfully crafted woman. The Bible records,

> The Lord God said, "It is not good for the man to be alone"....So the Lord God caused the man to fall into a deep sleep; and while he was sleeping, he took one of the man's ribs and closed up the place with flesh. Then the Lord God made the woman from the rib he had taken out of the man, and he brought her to the man (Genesis 2:18, 21-22).

It could be said that it was a "match made in heaven." The grandeur of the moment filled the earth when God escorted a beautiful wife to her husband. The two would become one, and a family was born.

A COURSE OF ACTION

Although marriage is God's idea, it often encounters devastating obstacles. Every relationship must realize that there are danger signs and warnings to navigate your marriage through the waters of trouble. The Titanic was warned on six separate occasions to change course, slow down, and take a southern route. The captain chose to ignore these warning signs, thinking his ship was unsinkable. On April 15, 1912, the Titanic sank after colliding with an iceberg, which ruptured five of its watertight compartments. Fifteen hundred men, women, and children perished.

If we are not careful, our marriages can resemble the Titanic. It may appear that all is well. The dangerous icebergs adrift seem to be distant and of no concern. The reports of impending danger are ignored. After all, "Our marriage is strong...isn't it?" Although a simple course correction would remedy the threat, it isn't until we are upon the iceberg of disaster that we choose to respond. Many times we respond too late.

It is important to discover the areas in your relationship that need change. Make a commitment with your spouse to make the proper course correction to avoid the icebergs of disaster. It often takes strength to change old habits and perceptions. However, your love will deepen and your relationship will strengthen, as you trust God for help.

AVOID THE ATTITUDE ICEBERG

The first course correction for a successful marriage is to avoid the attitude iceberg. When our relationships drift into troubled waters and come dangerously close to this iceberg, we develop attitudes and behaviors that emphasize the negative aspects of our marriage. We become preoccupied with every fault and imperfection. Every action of our spouse and others is magnified and scrutinized. I've heard it said, "The person who is always finding fault seldom finds anything else." Faultfinding is the "pebble-in-the-shoe" to a marriage. It causes a sore that is difficult to heal. It's not long before the blame game begins to rob us of joy.

My father would often say, "Son, you are responsible for your own happiness. No one can carry that burden but you." In other words, my happiness wasn't dependent upon friends or family. It was my responsibility. Gary Smalley has a simple formula to help you avoid the attitude iceberg:

> We can't change people.

> We can change ourselves.

> As we change, people around us adjust their responses and make decisions according to our new behavior.[45]

When we determine to make changes to help our marriage, our spouse will notice. It will cause them to make positive changes as well. It's important to dwell upon the positive and rewarding aspects of your marriage. Some people complain because God put thorns on roses, while others praise God for putting roses among thorns. Take time to notice the positive actions of your spouse...notice the roses among the thorns. Look for the good in your relationship and you will rediscover the deep satisfaction of being in love.

Avoid the Poor Communication Iceberg

Communication is to marriage what blood is to life. Developing excellent communication skills is absolutely essential to a healthy relationship. It is the vital ingredient for a fulfilling marriage. More couples suggest this as an area to improve their marriage than anything else. When communication is one-sided, it can be a bit comical, as suggested in this story of a judge preparing to hear a divorce case:

> "Why do you want a divorce?" the judge asked. "On what grounds?"

> "All over. We have an acre and a half," responded the woman.

> "No, no," said the judge. "Do you have a grudge?"

> "Yes, sir. Fits two cars."

> "I need a reason for the divorce," said the judge impatiently. "Does he beat you up?"

> "Oh, no. I'm up at six every day to do my exercises. He gets up later."

"Please," said the exasperated judge. "What is the reason you want a divorce?"

"Oh," she replied. "We can't seem to communicate with each other."[46]

It is important to listen to your spouse and hear what they are really trying to say. We become so consumed with getting *our* point across that we fail to hear *their* point. True communication is as much about hearing and comprehending as speaking. That is why God gave us two ears and one mouth. It is impossible to have any real relationship unless we are having real communication.

There are five levels of communication that are identified by most marriage counselors. These levels guide us through the superficial to the most meaningful moments in our relationship. A husband and wife who have learned to remain at the higher levels enjoy a more fulfilling and satisfying marriage.

FIVE LEVELS OF COMMUNICATION

Many of us begin our conversation at level one. This is known as the cliché or entry level in communication. "What's up?" "Not much!" "How was your day?" These are phrases that we often hear. They may come from our spouse, a friend, or a total stranger. At this level, conversation is safe and shallow.

We arrive at the next level when we add facts and information. Conversation may sound something like this, "Did you know that the St. Louis Cardinals beat the New York Yankees 5 to 3?" or "I hear they are building a new doughnut shop on the corner!" As you can see, this level is similar to level one. It is still relatively safe and shallow.

The third level takes us a little deeper into the waters of communication. It is here that real communication begins as we express our opinions and ideas. At this level, we might hear comments like, "Why is he running for the school board? He has no experience in education." We become vulnerable to criticism at this level. It is not as safe but reveals more of our own thoughts and ideas.

We find ourselves in the deep waters of communication at level four. It is here that we say what we feel, "I was hurt when my sister forgot my birthday." We run a risk of having our feelings misunderstood and misinterpreted at this level. However, our relationship will benefit from meaningful communication when we share our heart and feelings.

A couple needs to feel a sense of security in their relationship to reach level five. It is here that we reveal and express our need. It is important that the relationship be absolutely open, honest, and transparent to reach intimacy in communication. This may be difficult because of the risk of being rejected. However, the fruit of this level is a deep, loving, and enduring relationship.

Gary Smalley says, "The key to deep verbal intimacy is feeling *safe* to share our feelings and needs and feeling that our feelings and needs are *valued* by our mate."[47] This statement is extremely important to remember if we are going to experience a fruitful and meaningful relationship.

Communication goes beyond words and phrases. It is about truly understanding what is represented and perceived by our spouse. If we are to have real communication, we must understand the language of our spouse. For example, when a wife asks her husband to take out the garbage and clean the car, she is really saying, "If you love me, you will take out the garbage and clean the car." Often the husband doesn't perceive the request the same way. He simply hears the request and adds it to a task list. Because he doesn't attach the relationship to the tasks, he may get around to completing the tasks much later than the wife anticipates. This frustrates the wife who then perceives her husband's lack of timely response as a signal that he does not love her or care about their relationship. Generally this is not what the husband is meaning to convey, he simply does not understand his wife's love language.

FIVE LOVE LANGUAGES

Gary Chapman suggests that there are five ways in which people communicate love. It is what he terms the "love language."[48] These five languages are channels of communication in which a person expresses love. It is also the channel by which a person expects to receive love.

When I was younger, my father bought a CB radio. If we wanted to talk to truckers while traveling along the interstate, we had to turn to channel 19. Any other channel usually offered static. The same is true with our love languages. If we want to communicate in a way that our spouse will best receive our expression of love, then we must discover the channel through which our spouse receives and expresses love. Here are the five languages:

- Words of Affirmation—Verbal expressions of love.

- Quality Time—Companionship, doing something together.

- Gifts—Visual symbols of love.

- Acts of Service—Doing things for each other.

- Physical Touch—Caressing and touching as expressions of love.

Which of the five languages do you predominantly use to express and receive love? More importantly, which of the five does your spouse predominantly use to express and receive love? You should make it a goal to become an expert at speaking your spouse's love language.

Sometimes we can send wrong messages or signals to our spouse. These silent messages can cause confusion and frustration. We can say one thing while conveying and communicating something completely different. Marriage researchers suggest that there are three components of communication. The percentages below indicate how much of a message is communicated through each component.[49]

Content	7%
Tone	38%
Nonverbal	55%

We comprehend a higher percentage of nonverbal communication than content and tone combined. If we say something affirmative with our words while our body language conveys something negative, our spouse will interpret the nonverbal communication as the message we are trying to convey. If a wife asks her husband to go to the store to buy a gallon of milk and he responds by saying, "okay" while rolling his eyes, she is going to perceive that he doesn't want to go. It is important that the three components of communication work congruently to help us successfully communicate and avoid confusing messages.

AVOID THE UNRESOLVED ANGER ICEBERG

Unresolved anger is like an open wound that becomes lethal when not treated. Its devastation is evident in relationships that have been exposed to its poison. Unresolved anger affects families, friends, and marriages. Its most obvious symptom is the distance it puts in a relationship. Unresolved anger obstructs our channels of communication and blocks our ability to give and receive love. As a result, we feel distant and alienated from those around us and those we love.

God's Word expresses a concern about anger, "Everyone should be quick to listen, slow to speak and slow to become angry, for man's anger does not bring about the righteous life that God desires" (James 1:19-20). Anger hampers God's plan for your life. It stifles the spiritual growth and keeps us from being effective. The same is true in our marriages. Unresolved anger hampers and stifles the growth in our relationships and stalls any forward momentum in our marriage.

What is the root of anger? One of the best explanations I've come across is "unfulfilled expectations." It's not receiving what was expected. When we don't hear the words or receive the actions we expected, we become angry. When what we anticipate or wish does not take place, we become angry. We can become angry when something beyond our control happens, which may also lead to frustration and fear. If certain expectations are unfulfilled in a marriage, the seeds of anger and resentment will germinate and bear harmful fruit. Unresolved anger must be weeded and uprooted.

Although anger is not a sin, it's what we do when we're angry that can be sinful. In his letter to the Ephesians, Paul says, "In your anger do not sin: Do not let the sun go down while you are still angry, and do not give the devil a foothold" (Eph. 4:26-27). Paul is instructing the Ephesians to quickly resolve issues that have caused anger. When anger is not resolved, it robs us of joy and depletes our ability to nurture a healthy relationship. We then become vulnerable and are preyed upon by the enemy of our soul. It's in this atmosphere that we fall victim to actions that we regret later. To keep this from happening, we must take steps to resolve and unload anger.

First, acknowledge that you are angry and why you have been hurt. *Second,* try to look through the eyes of the one who hurt or disappointed you. It's important to make an effort to try to understand why your offender may have taken his or her course of action. *Third,* forgive and release your offender. It is here that true healing takes place and unresolved anger begins to dissipate. *Finally,* look for the good in the offense committed against you. Remember the Bible says, "All things work together for good to them that love God" (Rom. 8:28a KJV).

Avoid the Unmet Needs Iceberg

She was only four when she climbed into his lap. He had a large red suit with black buttons and a large black belt. His long white beard matched the white fur outlining his suit. Some called him Old Saint Nick, but to her he was Santa. Her brothers had asked for basketballs, skates, and candy. But when asked what she wanted Santa to bring her, our daughter, Alecia, timidly replied, "A Christmas tree and a checkbook."

Throughout the years, my wife and I have often remembered this precious memory with a smile. A checkbook seemed to be the answer to all of our daughter's wants and needs.

As a pastor I'm often asked, "What is the secret to a successful marriage?" With the divorce rate at record levels, people want to know the keys to making their marriage work. The operative word is *needs.* If you want to have a successful marriage, you must become an expert at meeting the needs of your spouse.

In the book, *His Needs, Her Needs,* Dr. Willard F. Harley reveals 10 of the most important marital needs of the husband and wife. He suggests that a couple will experience a relationship that sustains romance and increases intimacy if these marital needs are met.

The man's five most basic needs in marriage are:
1. Sexual fulfillment
2. Recreational companionship
3. An attractive spouse
4. Domestic support
5. Admiration

The woman's five most basic needs in marriage are:

1. Affection
2. Conversation
3. Honesty and openness
4. Financial support
5. Family Commitment[50]

The ability to meet each other's marital needs sometimes seems fleeting and elusive. Many couples struggle in their relationship to meet each other's marital needs simply from not being aware and identifying the needs. This is partly because we often fail to value and appreciate the needs of our partner. We find it difficult to relate to needs that are different from our own. In other words, his needs are not her needs. When we observe the two lists above, we find a remarkable contrast that suggests that men and women are different. When we seek to understand our spouse and observe the differences, we become equipped to fulfill his or her needs.

For the past several decades, our society has denied the fact that men and women are different. It has protested any suggestion of difference, fearing that one gender or the other would proclaim superiority. So to avoid the risk of being tarred and feathered, many marriage counselors said very little about gender differences. It wasn't until John Gray wrote his popular book, *Men Are from Mars, Woman Are from Venus,* that sanity began to return to our culture. Men and women are different! Not better or worse...just different.

It's important that men and women recognize and understand these differences. By embracing the diversity in a relationship, a couple actually becomes stronger. If two people agreed on every issue and thought exactly the same, one wouldn't be necessary. It's our differences that help us to make better choices and decisions. By understanding these differences and realizing that our spouse has different needs, we become empowered to meet those needs. We begin a process of preparing to meet their needs that we may not appreciate ourselves. Thus, we create a healthy and fulfilling marriage.

Avoid the Unresolved Conflict Iceberg

Dr. Howard Markman suggests that the divorce rate could be cut by more than 50 percent if couples would learn to resolve conflict.[51] In fact, marriage researchers can determine, with a 90 percent accuracy rate, whether a marriage will be successful or end in divorce by the way a couple resolves conflict. Resolving conflict is essential to a relationship. Our ability to negotiate the conflicts and challenges in marriage directly correlates to whether our marriage will survive.

Every relationship experiences conflict. Arguments and disagreements are a part of life. The important thing is how we resolve these conflicts. Healthy couples have learned to express disagreements in constructive ways, without tearing each other apart. In other words, they've learned to "fight fair."

There are five things that a couple should strive to avoid while working through an argument: criticism, defensiveness, expressing contempt, the "silent treatment," and the "divorce card."

Criticism tears a person down. It is always pointing a finger with an appetite to assign guilt. It is destructive to a relationship. On the other hand, a complaint can be healthy. It should express how a person feels without condemning the other.

Another area to avoid is *defensiveness*. Walls are constructed and the power windows go up when we are feeling attacked. However, this breaks down communication and repels the seed of truth that may have stepped on our toes.

Expressing contempt is extremely harmful to a relationship. Any belittling remark like, "Great going, Einstein!" or "Who made you God?" conveys a lack of value and respect for your spouse. It can also be demonstrated non-verbally. Rolling your eyes would be a good example.

Sometimes a husband or wife can give the "cold-shoulder treatment" (aka "the silent treatment") when entangled in a disagreement. This shuts off the flow of communication and endangers the relationship. Withdrawing from an argument only prolongs and delays a resolution. It is important to engage in the confrontation and work toward a solution.

The final thing to avoid in an argument is the *divorce card*. Too often couples play this card in an attempt to intimidate their spouse. Couples should refrain from making this type of threat when engaged in an argument.

A GOOD MEDICINE

There is a good remedy for an ailing marriage. It's called the marriage platinum rule, "Honor your spouse above yourself." Roman 12:10 says, "Honor one another above yourselves" and "be devoted to one another." It's a motto that should be lived as a lifestyle and a medicine that should be taken daily.

My oldest son loves baseball. Every waking minute is dedicated to pursuing excellence in the game. All he thinks, dreams, and talks about is baseball. He collects baseball cards, hats, and posters. He is more than just interested in the game—he is devoted! Pat Riley, former head coach of the L.A. Lakers basketball team, made this comment in his book entitled *Show Time*:

> Few people realize that beneath the surface glitter, the players bring a fanatical depth of preparation to every game. Their apparently spontaneous creativity and effortless innovation is actually the product of hundreds of hours of hard practice sessions. With that devotion to hard work, the Lakers have made a covenant with each other to put aside selfishness so that the team can achieve its goals, saying, "Whatever it takes for the team to win, I'll do it."[52]

If our spouse is a treasure sent from God, then we should have this same tenacity and commitment to our spouse and our marriage. We should be willing to say, "Whatever it takes for my marriage to win, I'll do it."

Every marriage has the potential to be successful. There is a key in every relationship that unlocks the door of intimacy and leads to a fruitful and rewarding marriage. Regardless of the challenges, if both the husband and wife will make a commitment to do whatever it takes to make their marriage work, then it will work. Many times it only takes a simple course correction to avoid the destructive marriage icebergs. It is God's plan for you to have a successful and fulfilling marriage.

Never underestimate the power of prayer. I heard recently that couples that pray together have less than a 1 percent divorce rate. It's true, couples that pray together—stay together. Dr. Nick Stinnett, a marriage researcher, found that there were six characteristics common to most happy marriages. One of the six characteristics was having an active, shared faith in God.[53] Your marriage has hope when you understand that God desires for you to have a healthy marriage that honors Him. With God, you can overcome any hurdle or obstacle. So, with confidence you can say, "For better or worse."

CHAPTER 10

For Heaven's Sake

Think of—
Stepping on shore, and finding it Heaven!
Of taking hold of a hand, and finding it God's hand.
Of breathing a new air, and finding it celestial air.
Of feeling invigorated, and finding it immortality.
Of passing from storm to tempest to an unknown calm
Of waking up, and finding it home.[54]

—Hazel Felleman

Have you ever found yourself asking the question, "Is this all that life has to offer?" Think about it...have you ever been consumed by the thought, "There has to be more to life than this"?

The apostle Paul had these same questions run through his mind. In his letter to the Corinthian church, he writes, "If in this life only we have hope in Christ, we are of all men most miserable" (1 Cor. 15:19 KJV), and the Living Bible says it this way: "If...[this is all there is], we are the most miserable of creatures."

There is, in the hearts of most people, an intense, sometimes unspoken, desire for the future world. Solomon wrote in the Book of Ecclesiastes, "He has...set eternity in the hearts of men" (Eccles. 3:11a). It's as if there is this magnetic pull to a place beyond the sky where dreams come true. Whether we want to admit it or not, heaven has captured our attention. Hollywood certainly understands this magnetic tug and creates movies to play upon this longing of our souls. We all remember Judy Garland, who mesmerized the world when she sang,

> Somewhere over the rainbow,
>   way up high,
> There's a land that I heard of
>   once in a lullaby.
>
> —*E.Y. Harburg*

While on vacation, I picked up an August issue of *Newsweek* magazine. The cover title, "Visions of Heaven," immediately caught my attention. As the article began to describe the different viewpoints of heaven from various scholars and clergy, a quote from author Sherwin Nuland captivated me. He said, speaking of heaven, "Even those of us who don't believe in one [heaven] sneakingly wish there was one."[55] His statement caused me to sigh. Those of us who have experienced Christ and believe the Bible as truth,understand that heaven is a real place. It is a continuation of life—a place that gives perspective to this world.

Hope is kindled and faith is ignited in knowing that life continues beyond the boundaries of an earthly realm. When tragic circumstances assault us, eternity becomes the balm that heals our deepest wounds.

Peggy Noonan, CBS News correspondent and speechwriter for Presidents Reagan and Bush, observes:

> I think we have lost the old knowledge that happiness is overrated—that, in a way, life is overrated. We have lost, somehow, a sense of mystery—about us, our purpose, our meaning, and our role. Our ancestors believed in two worlds, and understood this to be the solitary, poor, nasty, brutish and short one. We are the first generation of man that actually expected to find happiness here on earth, and our search for it has caused such—unhappiness. The reason: If you do not believe in another, higher world, if you believe only in the flat material world around you, if you believe that this is your only chance at happiness—if that is what you believe, then you are not disappointed when the world does not give you a good measure of its riches—you are despairing.[56]

It is imperative that we keep an eternal perspective. It's this eternal perspective that nurtures hope and keeps our faith alive. If we are not careful, catering to our immediate comfort and gratification can cause us to lose sight of eternity. Our eternal vision becomes blurry. Heaven becomes dim and distant in the everyday demands and hectic pace of our society.

Paul wrote to the Corinthians,

> *We can see and understand only a little about God now, as if we were peering at His reflection in a poor mirror; but someday we are going to see Him in His completeness, face-to-face. Now all that I know is hazy and blurred, but then I will see everything clearly* (1 Corinthians 13:12 TLB).

The trials and testing of our faith will one day make sense when we peer through the eyeglasses of eternity. We will understand the challenges of life clearly when we walk through the pearly gates of heaven. Unfortunately, our generation has ceased to embrace the relevance of eternity in everyday affairs. Although many believe in heaven, most live as though it doesn't exist. Most Christians want to be happier here—happier now. Face-lifts, tummy tucks, sculptured figures, fame, fortune, liposuction, and a myriad of other distractions keep us from the important. Many are so preoccupied with this world and its comforts that heaven has become merely a fairy tale.

OUR HOME ABOVE

The Bible encourages us to "set [our] minds on things above" (Col. 3:2a). We read in Hebrews that early Christians were preoccupied with the prospect that this world was temporal. It was a common belief that the injury of this world was temporary. "They admitted that they were aliens and strangers on earth...they were longing for a better country—a heavenly one. Therefore God is not ashamed to be called their God, for He has prepared a city for them" (Heb. 11:13b,16). Heaven, to the Early Church, was a glorious anticipation that brought balance to inequities in life. A.J. Conyers observes:

> As long as people were taught the idea...that our true home is elsewhere, there was a certain satisfaction in the answer itself. For centuries, the idea that this world is not, by itself, our home—emotionally, spiritually, or even socially—was a compelling idea because it was enormously convincing. It unlocked a secret about human existence that seemed to fit what everyone already sensed about human suffering, human aspirations, and the desire to

express life in self-giving love. Neither the flame of perse-
cution nor the ever-present danger of disease or war could
extinguish this new lease on life.

Poverty was still painful but not hopeless. Illness
might end in death, but death was not the absolute end. Life
took on a creative and vibrant energy because it was har-
nessed to an overall purpose.[57]

There is a bigger picture to life. It is beyond the boundaries and
parameters of this world. It is often referred to as the "Blessed Hope"—the
certain hope of Christ's return and our final, fulfilling home in heaven. This
hope yields purpose that propels us through the difficult moments in life.
Peter, speaking of this hope, exuberantly declares:

Praise be to the God and Father of our Lord Jesus
Christ! In His great mercy He has given us new birth into
a living hope through the resurrection of Jesus Christ
from the dead, and into an inheritance that can never
perish, spoil or fade—kept in heaven for you, who
through faith are shielded by God's power until the com-
ing of the salvation that is ready to be revealed in the last
time (1 Peter 1:3-5).

Notice that Peter refers to this hope as a living hope. This is the kind of
hope that consumes your heart, soul, and mind; a hope that is with you when
you wake up and when you go to bed. Peter continues by saying, "In this you
greatly rejoice, though now for a little while you may have had to suffer grief
in all kinds of trials" (1 Pet. 1:6) It's this assurance about the future, beyond our
difficulty, that gives us strength. Though life becomes difficult on this side of
eternity, we rejoice through our trials about what waits for us on the other side.

A young mother noticed her son reading the end of books before he
read the beginning. Inquisitively she asked, "Son, why are you reading the
end of the books first?"

He responded, "Because no matter how much trouble the hero gets
into, I don't worry because I know it's going to be all right in the end."

We should have the same confidence and assurance when facing the
difficulties and hardships in life. With our faith and trust in God, we
understand that everything is going to work out in the end. Heaven brings

a balance to the inequities we encounter here on earth. As Christians, we have hope in knowing the best is yet to come.

Jesus said,

> *Do not let your hearts be troubled. Trust in God; trust also in Me...I am going there to prepare a place for you. And if I go and prepare a place for you, I will come back and take you to be with Me that you also may be where I am* (John 14:1-3).

What a glorious promise to you and me!

LONGING FOR HOME

I'll always remember the day when my oldest son, Nathan, was born. It was a warm summer evening when I gently held him for the very first time. We immediately became best friends. I spent every spare moment, during the next several years, running, laughing, and playing hide and seek with my best little buddy.

During an extended trip, I called home to see how everything was going back at the ranch. After a brief summary of how things were, my wife said, "I've got to tell you what happened last night." She continued by saying, "Nathan and I took a calendar and circled the day when you were to return home. Each night we would scratch out a day and count how many days were left. Last night, after I put him to bed, I decided to see if he had fallen asleep. I noticed a glow coming from beneath the sheets, which he had also pulled over his head. As I pulled back the covers, I discovered that Nathan had indeed fallen asleep. It was then that I found him hugging his flashlight, with the light still on, in one arm and the calendar in the other. He had been looking at your calendar with the flashlight under the covers. I think he misses you."

As I listened to my wife relay what happened, my heart began to long for my son. I missed him, too. It caused me to take inventory of my life and ask, "Do I long for the return of the Lord like my son was longing for me? Is His imminent return causing me to gaze at the days on a calendar? Am I consumed with the thought that any day the trumpet will sound and we will see Jesus?"

We have become so busy that thoughts of eternity seldom cross our minds. We no longer have a preoccupation with our eternal home. Our lives have become so comfortable that heaven is a distant thought. And yet, the Scripture conveys that heaven is far superior to our best experiences on earth. Paul said to the Philippians, "I am torn between the two: I desire to depart and be with Christ, which is better by far" (Phil. 1:23). Heaven is clearly a part of Paul's thought process. His choices and actions are filtered through an eternal perspective.

This is not to suggest that God has called us to build a cocoon to isolate us from the responsibilities of this world, but rather to view the affairs of this world as temporal in light of the world to come.

BRINGING IT HOME

There are some questions that appear to have no answer. There are some events that seem impossible to explain. All of us face problems from time to time that are difficult to understand. Our lives are filled with dilemmas and challenges that seem unsolvable. And yet, God is greater than all of these problems and questions. He is able to solve the complex and impossible with the greatest of ease. When we look to God with these uncertainties, He sometimes chooses eternity as a means to fulfill His purpose in our lives.

God, who lives in heaven, sees all that transpires on this earth. He sees every offense, assault, cruelty, and injustice. His heart is broken with every hurt and injury. The wickedness of this world grieves the heart of God and kindles His wrath. Yet, because of His love and grace, His patience is vast toward man. It is His desire that everyone would turn from sin and repent of wickedness.

However, there is a judgment day coming. William Wadsworth Longfellow penned, "Though the mills of God grind slowly, yet they grind exceedingly small. Though with patience He stands waiting, with exactness He grinds all."[58] There is a day when the wrongs of this world will be made right and justice will be served. God will have the last word in the affairs of man. He will triumph! Knowing, then, that God will deal with our enemies in eternity, we are empowered to live in peace with the hope of our eternal home.

Joseph Stowell says, "Biblical hope is the forward-looking focus of our lives....In effect, we place our hope in a certain future event so compelling that it preoccupies our entire perception of life and, as such, radically alters our behavior in the process."[59]

My children look forward to visiting their grandparents each year. Playing with their cousins, riding horses, swimming, and driving go-carts intensifies their desire to visit. Throughout the year they live a normal life with the occasional question of, "When are we going to Grandma's house?" It's not until I specify a specific date that our lives become radically altered. Suddenly everything has changed. The dream has now become the great anticipation. They start planning, buying, and packing. This future event to visit Grandma and Grandpa's house now consumes their thoughts, impacts their decisions, and dominates their conversation. They talk non-stop about how much fun it will be when they get to Grandma's house.

This is an excellent example of biblical hope—the vibrant kind of hope that stirs all of us. It's this anticipation of Christ's return and the prospect of heaven that should dramatically change the way we live our lives.

Paul, speaking to the Roman Church notes, "For in this hope we were saved. But hope that is seen is no hope at all. Who hopes for what he already has? But if we hope for what we do not yet have, we wait for it patiently" (Rom. 8:24-25). When we apply hope to the unseen reality of heaven, our anticipation drives us to persevere through the most difficult of life's challenges. It's this eager anticipation that causes us to wait patiently. Regardless of the pressure and stress that we may be enduring, our resolve is firm because our hope is fixed on heaven.

When we take a closer look, in the biblical sense, at the word *hope,* we find it comes from the Greek root that means "trust." It is trusting God to keep His word. Our hope in heaven, which transcends reality, is all about trusting God. We live our lives trusting that God has prepared a place for us beyond this world. One day, we will experience this anticipation as a reality.

JESUS LOVES YOU

Has someone told you recently that Jesus loves you? It's true! His love for you led Him to Calvary. His resurrection is a statement of hope. He has ascended into heaven to prepare a place for you. This witness is true. He really does love you.

Several years ago I wrote a song to express Christ's love in my life. It's my "Amazing Grace." When I asked Jesus into my life, I immediately experienced His love, peace, and joy. My life was radically changed. I've spent a lifetime serving Him. Although there have been plenty of challenges along life's journey, I have discovered that Jesus has been a constant companion and friend. I have discovered that He is the reason I have hope.

You have hope, today, because Jesus loves you!

THE CALL OF LOVE

Has anybody ever failed the Lord,
Or is it that I'm the only one?
I strive so hard to be what I should be,
Forgetting it's Christ that lives in me.
I can't boast within myself
For I find no good in me,
Yet He loves me stubbornly as His own.
Where would I be if there never were a Calvary?
Where would I be if His grace had never reached to me?
For my life is not the same,
It was love that made the change;
And it's love that calls to you.
Love calls to me.
His grace still makes the vilest sinner clean:
The call of love
It's funny how I seldom give You time
When You're calling out to me.
But when I find the waves come rolling in,
It's You who calms my troubled sea.
Where would this poor sailor be
Without the Captain of the sea?
Where would I be without the Lord?
Where would I be if there never were a Calvary?
Where would I be if His grace had never reached to me?
For my life is not the same,
It was love that made the change;
And it's love that calls to you.
Love calls to me.
His grace still makes the vilest sinner clean:
The call of love.

CHAPTER 11

It's Just a Matter of When

As a songwriter, I've been able to write and arrange with some of the most creative people in the music industry. I have marveled at their ability to craft lyrics and carve out melodies that penetrate the deepest recesses of the soul. I've watched the symptoms of captivated people entranced by a song. The infatuation of the moment melts their heart and waters their eyes. A song has that capability. It can stop you in your tracks, put a dance in your step, or keep you from turning off your car until the final note. It's a well-crafted song that has an ability to inspire, encourage, and move us deeply.

Paul Bills, a good friend of mine, called me from his Nashville home excited about a new song he had just written. This is not too uncommon. Most writers, after completing a song, feel they have just written the next greatest hit. As I listened to his new song, I found myself immediately captured by the riveting lyrics and powerful melody. Its message soon became a medicine that started a healing process of rebuilding faith and hope in my life. Aaron Jeoffrey soon recorded this song entitled, "A Matter of When." Here are the lyrics:

> The time and the hour are all in His hands.
> When He makes a promise that's the place where I stand.
> He holds the future all in perfect time.
> I'm waiting for the impossible made by grand design.
>
> Some secrets of heaven are hidden from sight,
> To strengthen our faith in the love of Jesus Christ.

A love beyond reason it whispers to my soul,
"You don't have to live by what you see—God is in control."

It's just a matter of when a miracle will come.
It's just a matter of when—just look what He's done.
When dreams are born through a heart of faith placed in Him,
It's just a matter of when.[60]

It's not a matter of if, possibly, or maybe a miracle will happen. With our faith in God, it simply becomes a matter of when. God is able to reach beyond our boundaries to perform the unimaginable. He is a specialist at doing the impossible. He has a talent for accomplishing the supernatural. He lives in the realm of the extraordinary. He is known for the phenomenal. He is a God who does miracles.

He calmed the storm and hushed the sea. He walked on water and cursed a tree. He cast out demons and raised the dead while healing the sick upon their beds. He cured the lepers and touched the blind. He turned the water to the finest wine. The lame walked at His command as He healed the maimed and withered hands. He fed the crowds with fish and bread and "forgive their sin" is what He said. Jesus, the Son of God, significantly touched the lives of all who reached out to Him with a need.

The Bible is clear, "God shall supply all your need according to His riches in glory by Christ Jesus" (Phil. 4:19 KJV). There are times when your need requires a miracle. God used birds to feed Elijah in the desert during a great famine and drought. He sent manna to feed a nation journeying across the desert. Experienced fishermen, who had fished all night and caught nothing (see John 21:3), were told to cast their nets on the right side of the boat. Subsequently, the catch of fish was greater than their ability to haul it into the boat. When God says that He will *supply all of your need,* He is actually saying that He is your source. Your only real need is God. When Moses asked God, "What should I tell them is Your name?" God replied, "I AM WHO I AM" (Ex. 3:14). In other words, God was saying, "I AM the one who meets your every need; I AM the one who heals you when you're sick; I AM the one who lifts you up when you are down; I AM the one who feeds you when you're hungry; whatever your need—I AM."

How often we look to other sources rather than God to meet our need. I recently read, "If you want to be distressed, look within. If you want to be defeated, look back. If you want to be distracted, look around. But if you want to be delivered—look up!"[61] If you're in need of a miracle today, look up! If you're in need of healing, look up! If you're in need of an answer, look up! God is looking for an opportunity to show you what He can do. The prophet Jeremiah said, "Nothing is too hard for [God]" (Jer. 32:17b). Instead of looking through man's perspective, look up and view the situation through God's perspective. Anyone other than God will let you down.

Morris Plotts, a passionate missionary for God, told an incredible story of a plundering band of Mau Maus who surrounded and killed every inhabitant of the village of Lauri in 1956. Upon leaving the carnage, the Mau Maus headed immediately for the Rift Valley School that boarded missionary children. With clubs, spears, and bows and arrows, the Mau Maus set out to murder all the instructors and children in the school.

The glow from the Mau Maus' torches had already begun to light the night when word reached the school. It was evident that there would be no escape as they were completely surrounded. Though gripped with fear, the entire school looked to God and began to pray.

The Mau Maus began to curse and shout wildly. There seemed to be a cadence in each step of their advance. Their glistening spears and painted faces began to emerge from the jungle as the noose around the school began to tighten.

Suddenly, when they were close enough to overtake and destroy the school, the Mau Maus began to run for the jungle!

The local authorities and army were immediately called. They fanned out across the region and captured the entire band of marauders.

At the trial, the judge questioned the leader of the Mau Maus on the witness stand, "Were you the group that killed the inhabitants of Lauri?"

The leader responded, "Yes!"

The judge continued, "Was it your intent to do the same at the Rift Valley School?"

"Yes!"

The judge then asked, "What kept you from killing the students and teachers?"

The leader replied, "As we got closer to the school, many huge men dressed in shining garments with flaming swords suddenly appeared between us and the school. We were terrified and ran for the jungle."

God does work miracles. His promises are true. His favor rests upon those who trust in Him. It's this confidence in God that promotes hope in difficult circumstances and impossible situations. The last thing the enemy of your soul wants you to know is that the favor of God is upon you. He'll try to convince you that it is anything but God. It wasn't a coincidence that the Mau Maus ran back into the jungle—it was the miracle-working hand of God.

A HIDDEN MIRACLE

Sherri sang alto in our group, *Frontline.* Her ability to blend and harmonize with other singers was amazing. Not only did she possess a rare talent, but also was an integral part of our vocal ensemble.

It was quite a surprise when she came to me and said, "Nate, I'm going to have to leave the group for a while."

I asked, "Why?"

She said, "I have a growth on the back of my neck that seems to be getting worse. My doctor has recommended that I have surgery as soon as possible."

She then pulled her long beautiful hair to one side revealing the growth. It was shocking to see. It had been there for some time but was hidden by her long hair. The growth looked to be about half the size of an orange. It was disheartening to look upon.

I told her that I understood but felt God was going to heal her and use the miracle as a testimony. I then called the team over to pray. I noticed a tear fall from her cheek as we began praying.

A week later, Sherri came to me and said, "Nate, my parents are quite concerned. They have scheduled an appointment to have the growth removed in just a few days. I have no choice...I must leave. My father is planning to pick me up this afternoon."

I told her it was fine but once again felt compelled to say, "Sherri, God is going to heal you and use the miracle as a testimony."

I must admit that I was a little surprised at my comments. I knew God would touch her but to be so emphatic was not like me. I also understood that God sometimes chooses to use doctors and medicine to bring about healing. However, this time I felt different. I knew God and God alone was going to work a miracle.

Several days later Sherri caught up with us on tour. She said, "Nate, you won't believe what happened. I was prepped for surgery, waiting for anesthesia. The doctors decided to have one more look at the growth before they began to operate. While they were doing their final examination, they noticed that the growth was beginning to disintegrate right in front of their eyes. They canceled the surgery and told me to place a hot cloth on the growth once in the morning and once in the evening for about 15 minutes. About a day later, the growth had completely disappeared!" She then pulled her long beautiful hair to one side revealing the growth was gone.

No matter what you are facing, God is there for you. The Bible says, "Weeping may endure for a night, but joy comes in the morning" (Ps. 30:5b NKJV). Whatever you are going through, don't give up until you see the morning. It's at the end of every dark night and every broken promise. It's at the end of every betrayal, setback, and disappointment. The morning does come to dispel the night season in our lives. Joy will spill over into laughter when the light of God's compassion ushers in the dawn of new beginnings. His Word says, "His compassions fail not. They are new every morning: great is Thy faithfulness. The Lord is my portion...therefore will I hope in Him" (Lam. 3:22b-24 KJV). Hang on! Joy comes in the morning. It's just a matter of when a miracle will come.

A Mother's Prayer

Earlier in my ministry, I worked on staff at a church in Bellevue, Nebraska. It was a vibrant, growing church with many wonderful people. Part of my responsibilities, as a pastor, was to visit the hospitals and pray for the sick. Our church had a dry-erase board that listed those in our congregation who were in the hospital. On the days that I planned to visit the sick, I would write down the names with the corresponding hospital and room number.

One particular day, while writing down the names, I came across a gentleman who was dying of AIDS. In the comments field of the board it mentioned that he was not a Christian and did not attend church. Obviously, this caught my eye and touched my heart.

As I journeyed to the hospital with a friend, my heart seemed immensely heavy and burdened for this young man. As we walked into the room, I'll never forget seeing the shell of a man who seemed to be losing the fight with such a serious illness. It was evident that he had lost a considerable amount of weight.

Upon seeing us he said, "Who are you?"

After explaining that we were from a local church in Bellevue he said, "You're wasting your time."

I said, "Why is that?"

In a bit of a hopeless voice he responded, "You don't understand what I've done. I've done things so horrible that even God could never forgive me."

"Oh, but the good news is this," we said. "You are exactly the person that Jesus gave His life for. You were the reason that He went to Calvary and died upon a cross. You are the one Jesus loves!"

After a few more minutes of sharing God's love, he accepted Jesus Christ into his heart as his personal savior. Before we left the room he said, "My mother has been praying for me to ask Jesus into my life for years. I always had a hundred reasons to say no. I should have said yes a long time ago."

Our new friend in Christ died shortly after our visit.

The Senior Associate Pastor called me into his office the next day. He said, "The family has called and requested for the Senior Pastor to do the funeral, but he will be out of town this weekend. I also have a conflict that will not allow me to perform the funeral. Would you officiate?"

I thought to myself, "With all the other pastors on staff, why is he asking me?" It wasn't that I didn't want to minister to the family, I just felt less qualified. I accepted the offer and made arrangements to meet with the family.

As I walked into the room, I noticed the mother crying profusely. My heart was broken to see her grieving so. As I sat beside her, she cried, "I have been praying for nearly 20 years for my son's salvation and now he has gone into eternity without Christ. Reverend, why, oh why, didn't God answer my prayer?"

I said, "Oh, but God did answer your prayer." As she looked at me incredulously I continued, "You see, I was the one who led your son in the sinner's prayer as I visited him in the hospital. Although he was very sick, he asked Jesus into his heart. His only regret was that he hadn't made the decision to follow Christ much sooner." The mother's crying was then transformed into rejoicing. God had answered the fervent prayer of this mother.

If the Senior Pastor or the Associate Pastor would have performed the funeral, a mother's heart would not have been comforted and an answered prayer would have remained unknown. But God orchestrated the events to reveal His miracle at the right time and in the right place.

A Distant Relative of Job

As I've been writing this book, I have sensed that there are some who are at the point of giving up. You have struggled with the thoughts that miracles only happen to other people. Your frustration is only intensified when you hear of miracles that God has done for others. The light at the end of your tunnel seems to have flickered out and life has put you on hold. You are beginning to think that you're a distant relative of Job. Could this possibly characterize your feelings?

You can hear the cry and anguish of Job's heart in every word he spoke. Not that we could blame him. He was a casualty of a cataclysmic catastrophe. Everything that he had known or owned was destroyed. His cash crops were devastated. His livestock was decimated. His health had deteriorated. He was isolated in the death of his children and loved ones. His wife survived only to encourage him to "curse God and die." And yet, this was not all to his seemingly endless downward spiral.

Job was then visited by the four amigos. These compassionate friends had a talent for pointing fingers and assigning blame. Unfortunately, their fingers pointed to Job. He couldn't help but respond to their accusations and insinuations. His discourse craftily conveys a defense that is based upon his presupposition of God. He details, defines, and describes God's nature. You almost get the feeling that he knows more about God than God. For six consecutive chapters, Job steps up to the microphone and explains God. He even calls for an audience with God to answer him.

In the midst of grand debate, the unexpected happened. God spoke! Just when Job and his friends were catching their breath, God answered. This certainly caught everyone by surprise. The Bible records it this way:

> *Then the Lord answered Job out of the storm.... "Where were you when I laid the earth's foundation? Tell me, if you understand. Who marked off its dimensions? Surely you know! Who stretched a measuring line across it? On what were its footings set or who laid its cornerstone—while the morning stars sang together and all the angels shouted for joy?...Have you journeyed to the springs of the sea or walked in the recesses of the deep? ...Have you comprehended the vast expanses of the earth? Tell me, if you know this?"* (Job 38:1, 4-7, 16, 18)

God continues to shower Job with questions that declare His majesty, power, and glory. It's as if God is revealing His credentials to Job. God is greater than man's worst nightmare. He far exceeds human comprehension and intellect. He spans beyond the realm of human boundary. God's vastness is larger than our minds are able to imagine. Thus, God is uniquely qualified to do the impossible in Job's life.

There is a big difference between knowing of God and knowing God. Most people know of God. But how many of us really know God?

Job is left speechless. For the first time, he is at a loss for words, "I am unworthy—how can I reply to you? I put my hand over my mouth. I spoke once, but I have no answer—twice, but I will say no more" (Job 40:4-5).

We are so quick to speak out of frustration and to vent our disapproval at God. Our temporary unfulfilled expectations seem to justify our complaint. And yet, God's heart breaks at our lack of faith and understanding. He did not forsake Job and He will not forsake you. The Bible records this of Job, "The Lord blessed the latter part of Job's life more than the first" (Job 42:12a).

Listen, child of God, your latter will be greater than the first! Keep your hope and faith in God!

On October 8, 1871, a blaze began in Patrick O'Leary's cow barn on Chicago's West Side. The fire quickly spread resulting in nearly 200 million dollars in damage. It was the worst reported fire in Chicago's history.

A man who lost his shop in the fire went and surveyed the damage. He brought a table and a sign that he displayed in the ruins. It read, "Everything lost except wife, children, and hope—business will resume as usual tomorrow morning!"

Don't let the obstacles of this world keep you from accomplishing God's purpose for your life. With God there is always hope! A miracle will come…it's just a matter of when.

CHAPTER 12

God, Why Don't You Do Something?

Did you know the average person spends 5 years waiting in lines? What kind of lines? Subway station lines, amusement park lines, driver's license renewal lines, grocery checkout lines, ticket window lines, and the list continues, seemingly, infinitely. We spend 22 years of our lives sleeping, 14 years working, 6 years eating, 1 year searching for misplaced objects, 6 years watching television, 2 years returning calls, 8 months opening junk mail, and 3 years in meetings. Did you know that the average person spends 6 months at traffic lights waiting for the light to turn green? It frustrates me just to think about it.

My aversion to waiting started when I was a child. My mother would often say when I would ask her for a toy, "We'll see." In other words, "Not now—you need to wait." I hated that response. I didn't want to wait. I wanted the toy then and there. The phrase haunts me to this day.

I think most of us can relate. Life often thrusts us into periods of waiting. We find ourselves traversing the land of ambiguity feeling as though our life has been put on hold. It seems as though the sands of time are slipping through our fingers as opportunity evaporates. Waiting gnaws at our soul tempting us to respond prematurely—too often leading to poor choices. It's in such periods of waiting that we dangerously begin to reason, "We can't just sit around." This certainly proved to be Larry Walters' philosophy.

Larry was a truck driver who had tried on many occasions to become a pilot. Upon graduation from high school, he entered the Air Force in hopes of one day flying a jet. Unfortunately, poor eyesight grounded his hopes. His successive attempts also proved discouraging. For now, he would have to wait.

As he sat in his lawn chair watching jets fly overhead, his hunger to fly became a lure that led him to a crazy idea. Larry got in his jeep and went to the local Army-Navy surplus store and bought a tank of helium and 45 weather balloons. Not your average party balloons, but heavy-duty high-altitude weather balloons measuring four feet in diameter when fully inflated.

Larry's excitement to put his plan into action almost caused him to wreck his automobile on his way home. Like a kid with a new toy, Larry quickly assembled his contraption by strapping the balloons to his lawn chair. He then anchored his lawn chair to the bumper of his jeep and inflated the balloons with helium. With a few sandwiches and drinks, he was ready to take the matter of flying into his own hands.

Larry sank comfortably into his lawn chair and cut the rope. Like a silent rocket, he was propelled 11,000 feet into the air. Petrified with fear, he could only hang on and pray. For nearly 14 hours, he drifted lazily across the stratosphere until finally being spotted by a Pan-Am pilot who was making his approach at Los Angeles International Airport. The pilot radioed the tower about passing a guy sitting in a lawn chair at 11,000 feet. That radio transmission certainly raised a few eyebrows.

The Navy was quickly dispatched. As the rescue helicopter made its approach, the prevailing wind from the propeller blades pushed Larry in his homemade apparatus farther away. Eventually, they were able to hover over him and drop a rope. The rescue was successful.

As soon as Larry Walters touched ground, he was arrested. As he was being led away in handcuffs, a reporter yelled out, "Larry, why did you do it?" Larry paused for a moment and said, "A man can't just sit around."

Waiting can be frustrating. It certainly can lead a person to a decision they'll regret later. But most of the time, it causes us to question why we must wait.

A QUESTIONABLE MATTER

Have you ever been tired of waiting? Have you ever felt that your prayer wasn't heard? Have you ever cried out to God and asked, "Why don't You do something?" That's what the prophet Habakkuk did. This dusty itinerant man of God looked to heaven and cried, "How long, O Lord, must I call for help, but You do not listen? Or cry out to You, 'Violence!' but You do not save?" (Hab. 1:2)

It seemed Habakkuk's persistent warnings were falling on deaf ears. Right in front of his eyes, his tiny beloved nation of Judah was disintegrating. Judah was being sucked into a whirlpool of inevitable destruction through the wicked influence of King Jehoiakim. Habakkuk felt helpless. The waiting was too much. He clenched his fists, tightened his muscles, and lifted his head to cry, "How long! O Lord—How long, must I call for help, but You do not listen?"

Gideon could relate to Habakkuk's plight. He was hiding in a winepress from the Midianites when the angel of the Lord appeared to him and said, "The Lord is with you, mighty warrior" (Judg. 6:12). Gideon's response was, "But sir, if the Lord is with us, why has all this happened to us?" (Judg. 6:13a) In other words, "Why has God permitted the Midianites to destroy our homes, livestock, and crops? Why have they gotten away with looting our valuables, raping our women, and burning our camps? *Why has all this happened?*"

Martha could also relate. Her brother, Lazarus, had been ceremonially wrapped and buried in a tomb for four days by the time Jesus arrived. She had sent word to Him that Lazarus was sick, but He delayed in coming. When Martha saw Jesus, she cried out, "Lord, if you had been here, my brother would not have died" (John 11:21). In other words, "We waited, but You're too late! Why didn't You come sooner?"

Perhaps you can relate. Maybe, at some point in your life, you have asked these same questions. After all, you know what it is like to pace the floor at night. You've experienced the unbearable weight of the unknown. You've exhausted your entire repertoire of resources to no avail. You've prayed into the wee hours of the morning. Your friends attempt to encourage you by saying, "At this point, all you can do is wait." You succumb to the inevitable and ask, "God, why don't You do something?"

THE BIG PICTURE

Waiting time is not wasted time. God is doing something. You may not always see how God is working, but He is working. When God says, "All things work together for good to them that love God" (Rom. 8:28 KJV), He means "all things." Your circumstances are not unique. Your challenges are not different. You are not an exception to the rule. God includes you in the "all things work together for good" clause.

It can be difficult, at times, to understand how *all things* will work together for good. Too often we are betrayed by emotion and blinded by circumstances. The big picture simply escapes us. From our vantage point, we find it impossible to see the benefit from the experience. Until we understand that God possesses the master plan, we struggle with life's cacophony of challenges.

I remember auditioning for the symphonic band in high school. The director handed me a sheet of music entitled, "Toccata and Fugue in D minor" by J.S. Bach (better known as the classic theme from *Phantom of the Opera*). As I sight-read, I thought, "This doesn't make sense." Either I was doing poorly in my audition, or the other parts of the orchestra were vital. It wasn't until later in the year when the entire band performed the song that the intricate beauty was appreciated.

We play a similar role. We are one instrument in the symphony of life. We are one voice in its chorus. We are one part of a bigger picture. God is the master craftsman working and molding us into a work of art.

When we don't understand what God is doing, we often ask questions like why or how long. We want God to react immediately to our situation. First of all, God does not react—He acts! His plan for the ages has not been knocked off course. Our pressure points today will not change the way He directs history. God knows what He is doing. His ways are higher than ours. This is made clear in the writings of Isaiah:

> *For My thoughts are not your thoughts, neither are your ways My ways, saith the Lord. For as the heavens are higher than the earth, so are My ways higher than your ways, and My thoughts than your thoughts"* (Isaiah 55:8-9 KJV).

We may not always understand what God is doing, but we can trust that He is working all things for our good.

WAITING WITH PURPOSE

Dan Betzer, the speaker for the "Revivaltime" radio broadcast, would often say, "God is Sovereign!" The bottom line word in all theology is *sovereignty*. God can do anything with you He wants to do anytime, anywhere, under any circumstances that would be consistent with His divine nature that would ultimately make Him happy. The Book of Revelation says, "…for Thou hast created all things, and for THY pleasure they are and were created" (Rev. 4:11 KJV). In other words, you and I are a coin in the Master's hand to be spent anytime, anywhere, anyplace He so desires.

God's sovereignty affirms that He is absolutely in control. When you find yourself assailed by doubts and pummeled by questions, you can rest in knowing God is in control. When you are weak, He is strong. When you are lost, He knows the way. When you are afraid, He is courageous. When you fail, He forgives. When you are persecuted, He defends. When you fall, He's there to catch you. God is in control. Ira Stanphill, the great hymn writer penned, "I don't know about tomorrow; but I know who holds tomorrow."[62]

Even when we understand that God is in control, it's still difficult to submit to periods of waiting. When Potiphar threw Joseph into prison, he didn't rejoice and say, "This is the break I've been waiting for." Sometimes waiting is hard. It grinds at the soul like sandpaper. But all great men and women have experienced long periods of waiting.

Moses spent 40 years in the desert shoveling sheep dung waiting on God. There wasn't a corporate headhunter anywhere that would have given two cents for his future. But Moses learned to recognize God's voice in that period of waiting. He learned to trust God for his every need. He would use that experience to lead the nation of Israel out of Egyptian bondage.

David was called to be the next king of Israel. The prophet Samuel had anointed him with oil affirming his calling—but he's in a cave, hiding like a fugitive, fearing for his life. King Saul is scouring the Palestinian desert seeking his demise. In the recesses of the dark, arid cave, he wonders, "Where is God in all this?" David would live as a fugitive for another 13 years before ascending the thrown and becoming one of history's greatest kings. It happened as a result of waiting on God.

Although the waiting periods of life can be brutal, it is often the process God chooses to mold and shape you for greatness. Noah waited 120 years before the flood waters descended. Elijah hid 3 years in a ravine called Cherith while being fed by ravens. Paul was hidden away for 3 years in Arabia before embarking in ministry. John the Baptist spent most of his adult life preaching to the rocks in the wilderness. How many of us would line up for that assignment?

Waiting can sometimes seem prolonged and perilous. Listen, you are too important to be destroyed by a situation that was only meant to build integrity and character. Sustained periods of preparation fuel your effectiveness and develop maturity. You must understand the purpose for waiting or you'll live a life filled with frustration. While you wait, God works.

It's important to understand that waiting is the bridge that carries you from the will of God to the promise of God. Just as bridges come in different lengths, so does the bridge that carries you from God's will to God's promise. There are times, while crossing the bridge of patience, when it seems God's promise is slow in coming. You may even be tempted to believe that God's promise will never come—but keep crossing the bridge. Remember Abraham? Although he was old, he continued to believe and God fulfilled His promise in the birth of Isaac. His promises will always come to those who wait and trust Him.

The Bible ascribes great value in waiting. Here are a few verses that you need to read and remember.

> *Wait for the Lord; be strong and take heart and wait for the Lord* (Psalm 27:14).

> *Be still before the Lord and wait patiently for Him* (Psalm 37:7a).

> *Wait for the Lord and keep His way. He will exalt you to inherit the land* (Psalm 37:34a).

> *I waited patiently for the Lord; He turned to me and heard my cry* (Psalm 40:1).

> *Wait for your God always* (Hosea 12:6c).

The sacred pages of God's Word are filled with many verses that encourage us to wait, rest, or be still. The word *hurry,* however, would be difficult to find.

GOD'S RESPONSE

Habakkuk had the same problem you and I do. He couldn't see the big picture and he was tired of waiting. "How long, O Lord, must I call for help?" (Hab. 1:2) The question is reminiscent of what children might ask on a long trip, "How much longer to Grandma's house?" At least my children seem to ask that question a few—hundred times.

Just as we might answer our children, God answers Habakkuk.

Look at the nations and watch—and be utterly amazed. For I am going to do something in your days that you would not believe, even if you were told. I am raising up the Babylonians, that ruthless and impetuous people, who sweep across the whole earth to seize dwelling places not their own (Habakkuk 1:5-6).

Although Habakkuk had no way of knowing, God was doing something! His plan to resolve the blatant sin and corruption of Judah would be swift. An army, indeed, was amassing on the distant horizon. It would invade the tiny nation of Judah, like a hot knife through butter, and strip it of all its wealth and resources. Tens of thousands of Jewish captives would be chained together and carried off as slaves to Babylon.

Among those making the long trek eastward was a teenage boy named Daniel. As he faced the blistering sun in his pilgrimage toward Babylon with his beloved city of Jerusalem behind him, he must have asked, "God, why don't you do something?" But God had a tremendous plan for Daniel. For nearly 70 years, Daniel would be an aide and confidant to the greatest kings of antiquity. He would advise such kings as Nebuchadnezzar, Nabonidus, and Belshazzar. He would counsel such rulers as Cyrus and Darius. He would significantly impact history in a way that would never have been possible had he remained in Jerusalem. God was doing something.

Like Habakkuk, Gideon had trouble seeing the big picture. He was betrayed by his emotion and blinded by the circumstances. Remember

Gideon said, "If the Lord is with us, why has all this happened to us?" (Judg. 6:13) Notice, Gideon is conveying his immense frustration and hurt in asking such a question. In other words, "Lord, if You were really with us, then all of these terrible things wouldn't have happened." He continues his emotional wailing by adding, "But now the Lord has abandoned us..." (Judg. 6:13).

The Lord responds, "Go in the strength you have and save Israel out of Midian's hand. Am I not sending you?" (Judg. 6:14) The Lord instructs Gideon and then answers his sarcastic question with a rhetorical question: "Am I not sending you?"

Although this response soothes Gideon's emotional concern, he is now fearfully aware of his circumstances. "But Lord, how can I save Israel? My clan is the weakest in Manasseh, and I am the least in my family" (Judg. 6:15).

The Lord answers, "I will be with you, and you will strike down all the Midianites together" (Judg. 6:16).

When I was a boy, my mom would often say, "Nate, you and God are a majority." To this day, I find encouragement in those words. In essence, this is the message the Lord is conveying to Gideon. When God is on your side, who can be against you? Later we discover that Gideon took only 300 men and decimated the entire Midianite army. What a victory! This incredible feat has been recited countless times throughout the centuries. God was doing something.

Like Habakkuk and Gideon, Martha also had trouble seeing the big picture. From her vantage point, it was too late. That's why she cried, "Lord, if You had been here, my brother would not have died" (John 11:21). Even when Jesus told her, "Your brother will rise again," she still didn't grasp what He was telling her. She heard what He said, but never heard the message. Her posture of "it's too late" kept her from anticipating a miracle.

Jesus then proclaims to her, "I am the resurrection and the life. He who believes in Me will live, even though He dies; and whoever lives and believes in Me will never die. Do you believe this?" (John 11:25-26) Martha then replies, "Yes, Lord."

As Jesus arrives to the tomb, He requests for the stone to be rolled away. Again, Martha's "it's too late" posture begins to dominate. She says,

"But Lord, by this time there is a bad odor, for he has been there four days." Jesus replies, "Did I not tell you that if you believed, you would see the glory of God?" Jesus then prays, "Father, I thank You that You have heard Me. I knew that You always hear Me, but I said this for the benefit of the people standing here, that they may believe that You sent Me." When He finished, He called in a loud voice, "Lazarus, come out!" (John 11:39-43). And the Bible records that the dead man came out. How remarkable! God was doing something.

YOUR TIME HAS COME

How many times have you missed out on a miracle because you felt it was too late? How many times have you submitted to defeat because it was too difficult to see victory? The prophet Ezekiel wrote, "...None of My words will be delayed any longer; whatever I say will be fulfilled, declares the Sovereign Lord" (Ezek. 12:28). It's in those moments of hopelessness that you need to lift your voice and praise God. God has a delivery date scheduled for you. The day of waiting is over. God is about to answer your prayer.

When they chained Peter to the guards and carried him to his cell, it looked like it was too late. Herod had just butchered James a few days earlier. When Herod saw how much it pleased the Jews, he embarked upon a killing spree. The Church could only pray. Around the clock they buried their faces and called upon God to save their friend.

Little did they know, that as they prayed, God summoned an angel to rescue Peter. The angel slipped passed the guards, released the chains, and opened the city gates without notice. The angel then ushered Peter to the very home where his friends were praying. It was the first express carrier delivery ever recorded in history.

When Peter knocked on the door, the servant girl was so ecstatic to see Peter that she failed to open the door. She ran to the group and shouted, "Peter is at the door!" In disbelief they responded, "You're out of your mind." When she kept insisting that it was so, they said, "It must be an angel." Finally, when they opened the door and saw it was Peter, the Bible records, "They were astonished" (Acts 12:13-16).

Maybe you can relate to Peter's friends who were praying but not believing. They were locked in a posture of asking—but not expecting. Could it be that you're in the same vulnerable position? You're expectations have dwindled to nothing. In fact, you may have reasoned that it's too late. God is saying to you today, "The answer is right outside your door, get up and go open it." God's miracle for your life is about to happen. Expect great things and lift your voice in praise!

When Paul and Silas were shackled inside the damp, dark cell of a prison, their first response was to praise God. Why?—Because praise fills the heart with hope. Hope then becomes the soil in which the seed of faith germinates. And where there is faith, there are miracles. Faith touches the very heart of God. It moves Him into action. In fact, "without faith, it is impossible to please God" (Heb. 11:6a).

As Paul and Silas prayed and sang praises to God, the Bible records, "Suddenly, there was such a violent earthquake that the foundations of the prison were shaken. At once all the prison doors flew open, and everybody's chains came loose" (Acts 16:25-26). It wasn't until Paul and Silas began praising God that their chains fell powerless and their prison cell couldn't hold them. What is binding and holding you today? What is keeping you from reaching your miracle?

The Bible says, "Sing and make music in your heart to the Lord, always giving thanks to God the Father for everything, in the name of our Lord Jesus Christ" (Eph. 5:19b-20). Let praise lift you up when things appear hopeless. As you pray and sing, expectation will fill your heart and God will do something great in your life. Start praising God and watch what happens.

When Joshua wanted the walls to fall, after marching around Jericho seven times, God told him to give a loud shout. When he and all the people shouted, the walls of Jericho crumbled to the ground. Don't wait for the walls to fall to begin praising and shouting. Start praising and shouting and watch the walls crumble.

The Imperials recorded a song that says it best:

> Praise the Lord
> When you're up against a struggle
> That shatters all your dreams,
> And your hopes have been cruelly crushed

By Satan's manifested schemes,
And you feel the urge within you
To submit to earthly fears,
Don't let the faith you're standin' in
Seem to disappear.
Now Satan is a liar
And he tries to make us think
That we are paupers when he knows himself
We're children of the King.
So lift up the mighty shield of faith,
For the battle has been won.
We know that Jesus Christ is risen,
And the work's already done.

Chorus
Praise the Lord,
He can work through those who praise Him.
Praise the Lord,
For our God inhabits praise.
Praise the Lord,
For the chains that seem to bind you,
Serve only to remind you,
That they drop powerless behind you
When you praise Him.[63]

Peter wrote, "Let Him have your worries and cares, for He is always thinking about you and watching everything that concerns you" (1 Pet. 5:7 TLB). What a refreshing source of strength. In those periods of waiting, praise the Lord. In those hours of testing, praise the Lord. In the face of adversity, praise the Lord. God is watching everything that concerns you. He is doing something—just wait and see.

God Never Panics

The freezing temperature, the wet clothes, his shivering body and chattering teeth with the occasional sniffles, not to mention the shock of falling through the ice, caused my brother, Tom, to desperately long for home. After fishing him from the freezing waters of our favorite swimming hole that had thinly iced over, we helped him toward home. The short distance seemed to stretch beyond endurance for my six-year-old brother. His numbing body and stinging nose only added to his agonizing trek. If he could only get home, things would be okay.

The story may sound familiar. It's from the Preface at the beginning of the book. Now that you've finished reading the book, it's time to share the rest of Tom's story. I think it only appropriate to focus on what waited for him at home. It will encourage you to press on, if you are on the verge of quitting. It will encourage you to keep going, if you feel as though you'll never get home. It will encourage you to reach for home. And you will reach home! It's great when you get home.

Tom made it! He knew he was home when the arms of Mom wrapped around him and carried him toward a warm bath. She wiped away his tears and showered him with kisses. As he thawed in the warm waters, Mom began cooking his favorite soup—chicken noodle. She dressed him in warm dry clothes and ushered him to the table snuggled in a blanket. He was home! Life was fine now that he had made it through such a traumatic ordeal.

Listen, you'll make it, too! The day will come when you will laugh again! Life will be fine when you make it to the other side of your ordeal. Remember, the storm will pass. It is only for a season. Soon you will experience the warmth of God's grace flowing through your life. You will be nourished from the feast that God has prepared just for you. Your flickering hope will be transformed into a blazing reality of God's blessing. Just keep going and never give up!

Reading this book may have taught you about hope, but all this knowledge will amount to nothing unless it is translated into action. There are 10 action steps that I follow when confronting hopeless situations. These action steps are extremely helpful through the seasonal storms of life. If you are facing a crisis, let me encourage you to take action. Use these steps as a weapon to combat discouragement and despair. Never allow the flame of hope to flicker out.

Start by asking God for help. The Bible says, "Call to Me and I will answer you and tell you great and unsearchable things you do not know" (Jer. 33:3). Too often we wait until everything and everyone else has failed us before we turn to God for help. Take some time to kneel and pray. All the answers you need are discovered in time spent with God.

Surround yourself with friends who will inspire hope. This may mean giving up a relationship that is negative and discouraging. In times of crises, you need a friend who will encourage you in the Lord. Proverbs says, "A friend loves at all times" (Prov. 17:17a). No matter how dim the circumstances, a friend will fan the flame of hope.

Sing a song or chorus that expresses the majesty of God. Find a song that exalts the Lord and encourages your spirit. Make it your theme song and sing it often. God's Word says, "Sing to the Lord, praise His name; proclaim His salvation day after day" (Ps. 96:2). It also says, "Sing and make music in your heart to the Lord, always giving thanks to God the Father for everything, in the name of our Lord Jesus Christ" (Eph. 5:19b-20).

Reserve time for refreshing. Jesus would often retreat from the crowd to be refreshed. "After He had dismissed them, He went up on a mountainside by Himself to pray" (Matt. 14:23a). All of us from time to time need to get alone for a time of refreshing. Take walks on the beach or in the park. Retreat from your hectic schedule and allow time for refreshing and healing. It's in your quiet time that God often encourages you.

Read and memorize God's Word. David said, "I have hidden Your word in my heart" (Ps. 119:11a). Listen to this: "He sent forth His word and healed them" (Ps. 107:20a), "Now ye are clean through the word" (John 15:3a KJV), "Faith cometh by hearing, and hearing by the Word of God" (Rom. 10:17 KJV). God's Word will comfort, heal, guide, encourage, counsel, and help you with a myriad of challenges. Read the Word and highlight verses that encourage your soul. God uses His Word to build faith in your life. Tape those verses to your mirror, car, desk, refrigerator, or any place that will remind you of God's power and faithfulness.

Begin a spiritual growth plan for your life. Set a goal of reading one Christian book a month. Include in those selections Bible studies and workbooks. Paul instructed Timothy, "Study to show thyself approved unto God, a workman that needeth not to be ashamed, rightly dividing the word of truth" (2 Tim. 2:15 KJV). Reading introduces you to a wealth of knowledge that will help you mature in Christ.

Seek biblical counsel. It's important to seek and hear advice from the men and women of God. A pastor, Christian counselor, or Christian leader can offer valuable insight when facing the challenges of life. The Bible says, "The way of a fool seems right to him, but a wise man listens to advice" (Prov. 12:15).

Become active in your local church. Jesus said, "I must be about My Father's business" (Luke 2:49 KJV). We often discover God's purpose for our lives when we become active in His work. It's in helping others that we ourselves are helped. Use the talents God has given you. If you sing, join choir. If you teach, become a Sunday school teacher. Whatever your talent may be, get involved. Hear the words of Jesus, "Son, go work to day in My vineyard" (Matt. 21:28b KJV).

Exercise and eat right. "Honor God with your body" (1 Cor. 6:20b). It is important to eat well and exercise. Feeling better physically will energize you to be more productive. It will also give you a better disposition in tackling the tough problems of life.

Give your problem to God. This is absolutely the most difficult of the 10 steps. We simply have a hard time letting go. The Bible encourages you to "Cast all your anxiety on Him because He cares for you" (1 Pet. 5:7). Let it go! Determine to leave it in God's hands. Don't worry any longer. God can do more in five seconds than you can in five years. Letting go requires faith and trust. Trust God to do the impossible in your life.

The disciples were discouraged and in the process of quitting. The Bible records, "He [Jesus] saw at the water's edge two boats, left there by the fishermen, who were washing their nets" (Luke 5:2). Why were the fishermen washing their nets? The simple answer: They were quitting! Fishing wasn't working, so they were quitting.

Jesus told Simon, "Put into deep water, and let down the nets for a catch."

Simon answered, "Master, we've worked hard all night and haven't caught anything" (Luke 5:4-5).

I've fished with those guys before. And maybe you have, too. I think most of us have been where the disciples were—exhausted and beaten. They began to believe that the way things were, was the way things would always be. Their choice was clear—time to start washing nets.

Jesus loves to show up when you are on the brink. He walks into the middle of your problem and asks you to let go and trust Him. The question is will you obey?

Notice what happened when the disciples obeyed, "When they had done so, they caught such a large number of fish that their nets began to break" (Luke 5:6).

You may be washing your nets today, but it's not over. You may be on the verge of quitting, but don't give up. A miracle is just around the corner. God has a great blessing in store for you. If He can fill the empty nets of the disciples, He can certainly handle your problem. Remember, *God never panics!*

End Notes

1 Robert Strand, *Love 101* (Green Forest, AR: New Life Press, 1993), p. 44.

2 "Male Despair Tied to Atherosclerosis," *Chicago Tribune,* August 26, 1997, sec. 1, p. 8.

3 Bob Benson, *In Quest of the Shared Life* (Hermitage, TN: Generoux Publishers, 1986).

4 E.M. Bounds, *E.M. Bounds on Prayer* (New Kensington, PA: Whitaker House, 1997), p. 122.

5 Richard G. Lee, *There's Hope for the Future* (Nashville, TN: Broadman & Holman Publishers, 1996), pp. 104-5.

6 Gary Smalley, *Making Love Last Forever* video (Nashville, TN: Word Publishing, 1997).

7 Al Kaltman, *The Genius of Robert E. Lee* (Paramus NJ: Prentice Hall Press, 2000), p. 151.

8 Kaltman, *Robert E. Lee*, p. 151.

9 U.S. Senator Robert G. Torricelli (ed.), *Quotations for Public Speakers: A Historical, Literary, and Political Anthology* (New Brunswick, NJ: Rutgers University Press, 2000), p. 1.

10 Torricelli, *Quotations,* p. 3.

11 Torricelli, p. 3.

12 Torricelli, p. 32.

13 Walter A. Maier as quoted from Charles R. Swindoll, *The Tale of the Tardy Oxcart* (Nashville, TN: Word Publishing, Inc. 1998), p. 23.

14 C.S. Lewis, *The Problem of Pain* (New York: Macmillan Publishing Co., Collier Books, 1962), p. 93.

15 A.W. Tozer, *The Root of the Righteous* (Camp Hill, PA: Christian Publications, Inc., 1986), p. 137.

16 Charles R. Swindoll, *Joseph: A Man of Integrity and Forgiveness* (Nashville, TN: Word Publishing, 1998), p. 59.

17 Torricelli, p. 46.

18 Torricelli, p. 229.

19 Rev. Robert Strand, *Take a Break* (Springfield, MO: Gospel Publishing House, 1992), pp. 8-9.

20 Robert Strand, *Moments for Teens* (Green Forest, AR: New Leaf Press), Day 3.

21 Janet Lowe, *Billy Graham Speaks* (New York: John Wiley & Sons, Inc., 1999), p. 39.

22 Torricelli, p. 47.

23 Swindoll, *The Tale*, p. 383.

24 Swindoll, *The Tale,* p. 548.

25 Swindoll, *The Tale,* p. 452.

26 Torricelli, p. 45.

27 Lowell Russell Ditzen, *The Storm and the Rainbow* (New York: Henry Holt and Co., Inc., 1959), p. 73.

28 Ditzen, *The Storm,* p. 73.

29 Charles R. Swindoll, *Paul: A Man of Grace and Grit* (Nashville, TN: Word Publishing Group, 2002), p. 153.

30 Jane Eggleston, "It's in the Valleys I Grow," retrieved from the Worldwide Web at: http://www.aspecialplace.net/PoetryCorner/its_in_the_valleys.htm

31 Lewis M. Smedes, *Forgive and Forget* (New York, NY: Harper & Row Publisher, Inc., 1984) p. 2.

32 Smedes, *Forgive,* p. 7.

33 Smedes, *Forgive,* p. 29.

34 Swindoll, *The Tale,* p. 216.

35 Edwin Evans, *Parables, Etc.* (Saratoga, CA: Saratoga Press, June 1984), p. 2.

36 Swindoll, *The Tale,* p. 476.

37 Torricelli, p. 41.

38 Denis E. Waitley, *Seeds of Greatness* (Grand Rapids: Revell, 1983).

39 John C. Maxwell, *The Success Journey* (Nashville, TN: Thomas Nelson, Inc., 1997), pp. 122-123.

40 David Neeham, *Close to His Majesty* (Multnomah Books, 1987), quoted by Alice Gray in *Stories for the Heart* (Gresham, OR: Vision House Publishers, 1996), p. 129.

41 William Bennett, *The Index of Leading Cultural Indicators: Facts and Figures on the State of American Society* (New York: Simon & Schuster, 1994), cited by David Haney in *A Living Hope* (Wheaton, IL: Crossway Books, 1999), p. 16.

42 Harry F. Waters, "Teenage Suicide: One Act Not to Follow," *Newsweek* (April 18, 1994), p. 49.

43 U.S. Department of Justice, Bureau of Justice Statistics.

44 Max Lucado, *In the Eye of the Storm* (Dallas, TX: Word Publishing, Inc., 1991), p. 200.

45 Gary Smalley, *Making Love Last Forever* (Nashville, TN: LifeWay Press, 1996), p. 10.

46 John Maxwell, *Developing the Leaders Around You* (Nashville, TN: Thomas Nelson, Inc., 1995), p. 58.

47 Smalley, *Making,* p. 131.

48 Gary Chapman, *The Five Love Languages* (Chicago: Northfield Publishing, 1995).

49 H. Norman Wright & Wes Roberts, *Before You Say I Do* (Eugene, OR: Harvest House Publishers, 1997), p. 57.

50 Willard F. Harley, *His Needs, Her Needs* (Old Tappan, NJ: Fleming H. Revell Company, 1986), p. 10.

51 Howard Markman, Scott Stanley, and Susan Blumberg, *Fighting for Your Marriage,* as cited by Gary Smalley, *Making Love Last Forever,* p. 169.

52 Pat Riley, *From Prologue to Showtime, Inside the Lakers' Breakthrough Season,* (Warner Books, 1988).

53 Nick Stinnett and John DeFrain, *Secrets of Strong Families* (New York: Berkley, 1986).

54 Swindoll, *The Tale,* p. 265.

55 Lisa Miller, "Visions of Heaven," *Newsweek,* August 12, 2002, Vol. CXL, No.7, p. 47.

56 Peggy Noonan, "You'd Cry Too," *Forbes,* September 14, 1992, p. 65.

57 A.J. Conyers, *The Eclipse of Heaven* (Downers Grove, IL: InterVarsity, 1992), p. 78.

58 Swindoll, *The Tale,* p. 323.

59 Joseph M. Stowell, *Eternity* (Chicago, IL: Moody Press, 1995), p. 62.

60 Paul Bills and Kevin Stokes, "A Matter of When" (copyright 1996 Shepherd's Fold Music /EMI Christian Music).

61 Bob Gass, *The Word for Today* (Roswell, GA: Bob Gass Ministries, Dec. 16, 2000-01), p. 29.

62 Ira Stanphill, "I Know Who Holds Tomorrow" (Copyright 1950 by Singspiration, Inc.).

63 Brown Bannister and Mike Hudson, "Praise the Lord" (Copyright 1978 by Word Music, Inc.).

How to contact us!

For comments, questions, or booking information,
please send E-mail to:
Godneverpanics@aol.com
Or visit
www.natecarter.com

Additional copies of this book and other book titles from DESTINY IMAGE are available at your local bookstore.

For a complete list of our titles, visit us at www.destinyimage.com Send a request for a catalog to:

Destiny Image® Publishers, Inc.
P.O. Box 310
Shippensburg, PA 17257-0310

"Speaking to the Purposes of God for This Generation and for the Generations to Come"